A Passion for Faithfulness

A Passion
for
Faithfulness

WISDOM FROM THE
BOOK OF NEHEMIAH

J. I. Packer

CROSSWAY BOOKS • WHEATON, ILLINOIS
A DIVISION OF GOOD NEWS PUBLISHERS

A Passion for Faithfulness

Copyright © 1995 by J. I. Packer

Published by Crossway Books
> A division of Good News Publishers
> 1300 Crescent Street
> Wheaton, Illinois 60187

All rights reserved. No part of this publication may be reproduced, stored in a retrieval system or transmitted in any form by any means, electronic, mechanical, photocopy, recording or otherwise, without the prior permission of the publisher, except as provided by USA copyright law.

Cover photo: Laurance B. Aiuppy / FPG International

Cover design: Cindy Kiple

First printing, 1995

Printed in the United States of America

Library of Congress Cataloging-in-Publication Data
Packer, J.I., (James Innell)
    A passion for faithfulness: Wisdom from the Book of Nehemiah / J.I. Packer
        p.   cm.—(A living insights Bible study: bk. 1)
    Includes bibliographical references and indexes.
    1. Bible. O.T. Nehemiah—Criticism, interpretation, etc. 2. Faith.
3. Loyalty   I. Title. II. Series: Packer, J.I. (James Innell). Living insights Bible study; Bk. 1.
BS1365.2.P33 1995   222'.806—dc20   94-24366
ISBN 0-891077-733-2

03	02	01	00	99	98	97	96	95
15	14	13	12	11	10	9 8	7	6	5	4	3	2	1

For
Fred and Elizabeth
in whom
so many of
Nehemiah's strengths
have reappeared

Contents

Preface
to the Series

Were not our hearts burning within us while he . . . opened the Scriptures to us?" So testified the two disciples with whom Jesus, risen from the dead, walked and talked on the first Easter Sunday afternoon (Lk. 24:32). The health-giving heartburn that they experienced was not unique to them; on the contrary, all those in every age to whom God's Word is opened know it. What is it? It is a blend of clarity and joy in the presence of God that excites one for worship, work, and witness. To further it is the proper aim of preaching; and that is the aim of the *Living Insights Bible Studies* too.

Living Insights Bible Studies are, in effect, preaching on paper. Each book takes a unit of the Bible and seeks to let it function as light from God to expose and direct. The biblical name for God's light functioning in this way is *wisdom*; hence the subtitles of the books. *Living Insights Bible Studies* are not commentaries: they are less, in that they do not try to cover everything, and they are more, in that they pursue key biblical themes to foster spiritual life.

Being thematic in character, the books begin by laying out the themes on which the expositions focus. This belongs to the design of the series and fixes each book's thrust.

I hope and pray that God will use *Living Insights Bible Studies* as a means whereby the exalted excitement of the Emmaus road may be renewed today.

J. I. Packer

Prologue:
Church-Building

For me to celebrate Nehemiah as a church builder and to urge this supremely as how Christians should regard him may raise some eyebrows. But that is what I shall do in this book, and I want to begin by explaining why. So now I glance back fifty years.

CHRIST LOVES THE CHURCH

He was an odd little man, lean, intense, and jerky, with a face that seemed to light up as he spoke. His dress was odd, too, by my undergraduate standards, for he wore a brown monastic habit, the uniform of an Anglican Franciscan. I was there out of loyalty to the college chapel, not expecting to be impressed; but he captured my attention telling us how in his teens he had experienced a personal conversion to Jesus Christ, like that which I had just undergone myself. "And then," he said, "I got excited about the church. You could say, I fell in love with it." Never had I heard anyone talk quite like that before, and his words stuck in my memory. Fifty years later, I can still hear him saying them. He then hammered home the point that all who love Jesus Christ the Lord ought to care deeply about the church, just because the church is the object of Jesus' own love. Church-centeredness is thus one way in which Christ-centeredness ought to find expression. Was he right? Yes, he was: no question about that.

For listen to Paul, instructing the Ephesians and others (there is good reason to regard Ephesians as a circular letter): "Christ loved the church and gave himself up for her to make her holy, cleansing her by the washing with water through the word, and to present her to himself as a radiant church, without stain or wrinkle or any other blemish, but holy and blameless" (Eph. 5:25-27). Now weigh the words of the hymn as it echoes this and other New Testament passages:

> *The church's one foundation*
> *Is Jesus Christ her Lord;*
> *She is his new creation*
> *By water and the word:*
> *From heaven he came and sought her*
> *To be his holy bride;*
> *With his own blood he bought her,*
> *And for her life he died.*

Next, observe that the glory, present and future, that God gives to "the bride, the wife of the Lamb" (Rev. 21:9), as the issue and end-product of his own great grace, is from one standpoint the central focus of the New Testament, reaching its climax in the envisionings of the true Mount Zion in Hebrews 12:22-24 and of the new Jerusalem (Rev. 21:1–22:5; see also Rev. 7, a further depiction of the church's destiny). And link with that the fact that "glory [here meaning, doxology and praise] in the church and in Christ Jesus throughout all generations, for ever and ever!" (Eph. 3:21) is the climactic focus of Christian religion—"in the church and in Christ Jesus" being two complementary phrases explaining and reinforcing each other. So the church that Christ loves and sustains is the key feature of God's plan for both time and eternity, and care for the church's welfare, which is what love for the church means, is an aspect of Christlikeness that Christians must ever seek to cultivate. We are right to take the church on our hearts; we should be wrong not to. For as proverbially we say to each other, "Love me, love my dog," so our Lord Jesus says to us all, "Love me, love my church."

It was clear from the way the little man expressed himself that he expected evangelical Christians to be concerned only about their own societies and fellowships, and to lack interest in what the early Fathers called the great church and the Westminster divines the catholic visible church—namely, the worldwide Christian community in its countless congregational outcrops. This expectation is still very common outside evangelical circles, and there have certainly been individuals whose sayings and doings have kept it in place. No doubt lack of concern about the church as such is the occupational temptation of any who seek to foster experiential personal faith in Christ in a minority situation, where most church leaders are not on the evangelical wavelength—a state of things that has unhappily been common in the Western world during the past hundred years. But half a century's observation has shown me that evangelical leaders and opinion-makers are not as a body marked by unconcern about the catholic visible church; rather the reverse. To pray and plan and pray again for the reforming and revitalizing of the church has been part of the mainstream evangelical way since the sixteenth century, and is so still—as indeed it ought to be. For the little man was right: something is wrong with professed Christians who do not identify with the church, and love it, and invest themselves in it, and carry its needs on their hearts. Evangelicals, the Bible-and-gospel, Christ-and-Spirit people spread through the denominations worldwide (and, incidentally, multiplying at a phenomenal rate just at present), must continue to model love for the church.

But how should such love be focused and expressed? Here, unhappily, the ways divide. For those many who equate the church with its institutional form, love for the church means enthusing over its liturgy, ceremony, bureau-cracy, and the labor that keeps its wheels revolving. Being more interested in maintenance and nurture than in mission and evangelism, folk of this kind are constantly indifferent, indeed often opposed, to any active concern for conversions and for non-institutionalized expressions of faith, in a way that evangelicals find distressing. For evangelicals think of the church in terms of the communal life that the institu-tional forms exist to canalize. They see the church as the Lord's people getting together on a regular basis to do the things that the church does—praise and pray, with preach-ing and teaching; practice fellowship and pastoral care, with mutual encouragement and accountability; exalt and honor Jesus Christ, specifically by word, song, and sacrament; and reach out, locally and cross-culturally, in order to share Christ with people who need him. Here love for the church finds expression in a constant quest for faithfulness, holiness, and vitality—ardor animating order—in the corporate life of communing with the Father and the Son through the Spirit that is the church's real essence. I had better come clean here and say straight out that the evangelical understanding seems to me to accord with the New Testament and will be assumed in all that follows.

CHRIST BUILDS THE CHURCH

Jesus Christ's own church-centeredness came out clearly on the first occasion when we hear of him using the word. It was at a turning-point in his ministry, when Peter as spokesman for the disciples had just answered Jesus' ques-tion, "Who do you say I am?" by declaring, "You are the Christ," God's appointed and anointed King, the true center of world history. Jesus' response was: "Blessed are you, Simon son of Jonah, for this was not revealed to you by man, but by my Father in heaven. And I tell you that you are Peter [the name means "rock"], and on this rock I will build my church, and the gates of Hades will not overcome it" (Mt. 16:15-18). We can bypass the disputes about Jesus' exact meaning, whether the church's rock-foundation is to be Peter's confession of faith as distinct from Peter himself, or Peter himself, the confessor, in the power of his faith, and whether "the gates of Hades" (some form of the power of death) should be thought of as attacking the church or as resisting attacks by the church or as both together. What matters for us is Jesus' statement that he, in person, will build a church that is his, and it will triumph over all the forms and powers of death. Let us try to see what that means.

When today we in the West speak of "our church," we are normally referring either to the *building* (a roofed meeting hall, auditorium, or worship space, sometimes towered or steepled, sometimes not) or to the *denomination* (a federation, loose or tight, of like-minded or at least like-mannered congregations for some form of mutual help). We call these entities "ours" because we have chosen to link up with them; "ours" signifies identification, not possession. But when at Caesarea Philippi, nearly two millennia ago, Jesus spoke of "my church," possession was central to his meaning. For what he had in view was a community unified and identified by a shared allegiance to himself—a common acknowledgment of his claim upon them and his Lordship over them, and a common bond of love, loyalty, and devotion to him.

"Church" in Matthew's text is *ekklesia*, the regular Greek word for a public gathering, which Matthew's Greek Old Testament, the Septuagint, regularly uses for the Hebrew *qahal*, "congregation." *Qahal* signified the Israelites met together in their official character as Yahweh's covenant people. Yahweh had formed Old Testament Israel by redeeming the people from Egyptian bondage and revealing to them the reality of his covenant. Jesus' thought clearly was that he himself would form a community bonded together by a common grasp of the reality that Simon Peter had just confessed—namely, that Jesus was the appointed and anointed Christ, the Son of God both officially and personally, the maker and master of all things, the Lord of all life, the determiner of all destinies, and the Saviour of all his servants. From him and his messianic ministry his church would derive its identity; to him in his messianic glory it would give its loyalty. It would be his church in every sense.

Nor would the founding of it be in any sense a breakaway from the past. On the contrary, Christ's church was to be, and now is, nothing more nor less than the Old Testament covenant community itself, in a new and fulfilled form that God had planned for it from the start. It is Israel internationalized and globally extended in, through, and under the unifying dominion of Jesus, the divine Saviour who is its King. It is God the Father's family, as appears from the fact that Jesus taught his followers to think and speak of his Heavenly Father as theirs too. It is the risen Christ's body and bride, destined for the ultimate in intimacy with him and the sharing of his life. It is the fellowship of the Holy Spirit, the unseen but potent divine facilitator who shows us that Jesus the Christ is real today, who sustains our trust in him and our love for him, who shapes and reconstructs our character in his likeness, and who supplies us with abilities for the mutual ministry that we sometimes call "body-life." ("Fellowship of the Holy Spirit" in 2 Corintians 13:14 appears to mean both "partnership with the Spirit" and "partnership with others that is brought about by the Spirit.")

In a word, the church is the community that lives in and by covenant communion between the triune God and itself. As the royal High Priest in God's kingdom of salvation and sanctity, Jesus laid the foundation for this relationship by his atoning death; now he actually mediates covenant communion to the community corporately, and to each participant individually, through the Holy Spirit and in the power of his own ongoing risen life. Such, then, was the reality Jesus had in mind when he spoke of "my church."

It is not likely that Simon Peter understood much of this when he confessed Jesus to be the Christ. Jewish exegetes at that time did not perceive that the Old Testament prophecies concerning the Christ coalesce in a figure in whom royal priesthood, suffering servanthood, and death leading to resurrection and enthronement all combine, and none of Jesus' disciples seem to have grasped this till after he rose from the dead. But Jesus, reading Simon's heart while listening to his words, discerned true trust and commitment—true faith, that is—going along with Simon's insight into Jesus' official role. It was as if Simon had said: "You, Jesus, are the one who is to bring world history to its final goal, whatever that may be; you are also the one who is to bring my personal history to its final goal, whatever that may be; I know that this is who you are, even though I don't know all that you may do; so I acknowledge you as the Christ and bind myself to you accordingly." To which Jesus responded by declaring that on this foundation of faith he would build his church.

What did he mean?

When we speak of building a church, our minds are usually on the bricks and mortar out of which the new structure will be constructed, and we say that it is being built by the architect who designed it, or the congregation or denomination or benefactor that financed it, or the construction firm that is putting it up. But when Jesus spoke of building his church, he was not thinking in those terms. He was thinking, rather, of the complex process whereby the truth about himself is received, the recipients respond to it (or, better, respond to him in terms of it, as Peter was doing), and the responders are conformed increasingly to him as they share in the things that the church does in obedience to Jesus' word, under his leadership, and in dependence on his power. As the church consists of individuals who by coming to faith and associating as believers have become the Lord's people (his vine, his flock, his temple, his nation), so Christ's building of the church is a matter of his so changing people on the inside—in their hearts, as we say—that repentance, faith, and obedience become more and more the pattern of their lives. Thus increasingly they exhibit the humility, purity, love, and zeal for God that we see in Jesus, and fulfill Jesus' call to worship, work, and witness in his name. And this they do, not as isolated individuals (lone-rangerism!), but as fellow-siblings in God's family, helping and encouraging each other in the openness and mutual care that are the hallmarks of "brotherly love" (*philadelphia*: see Rom. 12:10; 1 Thess. 4:9; Heb. 13:1; 1 Pet. 1:22; 2 Pet. 1:7). Hereby they enter increasingly into the life that constitutes authentic Christianity, the life of fellowship with their Heavenly Father, their risen Saviour, and each other; and in so doing they are "built into a spiritual house to be a holy priesthood, offering spiritual sacrifices acceptable to God through Jesus Christ" (1 Pet. 2:5).

So "I will *build* my church" is a metaphor, just as Jesus' earlier promise to Simon, "from now on you will be *catching* people" (Lk. 5:10, NRSV) was a metaphor. In the latter case, Jesus was comparing Simon's forthcoming work as a disciple-maker with his use of his current skill as a fisherman. In the present case, he is telling Peter that his own gracious work of new-community-building would be comparable to that of a contractor putting up a house by bonding together raw materials (stone, bricks, planks, logs) that had been gathered for that purpose. His immediate point in the sentence where the metaphor occurs is that the rock-foundation on which the community is to stand—that is, the basic commitment that each person bonded into the church must share—is the faith in himself as divine Messiah that Peter had just verbalized: "*on this rock* I will build my church." The building process itself, however, is what concerns us now.

THE WORD AND THE SPIRIT

By what means does the Saviour build his church? That is, how does he bring about the changes in people that weld them in this ever-deepening way into the worship-and-service team of active believers for which "church" is the biblical name? The answer is: through his Word (in the broadest sense, the Bible; in sharper focus, the gospel), and by his Spirit, whose role in this connection is to make the meaning and application of the Word clear and personal. Word and Spirit together, the Spirit interpreting and evoking response, are the means whereby Christ's church-building work (*edification*, as English versions of the Bible usually render it) is carried forward.

Paul in Ephesians pictures this process as church *growth*. Having explained that Christ gives gifted servants to the church "to equip the saints for the work of ministry, for *building up* the body of Christ, until all of us come to the unity of the faith and of the knowledge of the Son of God," he affirms that by this means we are to "*grow up* in every way into him who is the head, into Christ, from whom the whole body, joined and knit together by every ligament with which it is equipped, as each part is working properly, promotes *the body's growth* in *building itself up* in love" (Eph. 4:12-16, NRSV). Thus Christ "holds the whole building together and *makes it grow* into a sacred temple dedicated to the Lord. In union with him you too are being *built together* with all the others into a place where God lives through his Spirit" (Eph. 2:20-21, GNV).

In light of Paul's picture of the church growing as a body grows and as a building grows through the process of its erection, it seems regrettable that the phrase "church growth" should nowadays be used exclusively, as it seems to be, of numerical expansion, when the New Testament idea expressed by this phrase is not of quantitative but of qualitative advance. It is always wisest to use biblical phraseology in its biblical sense, and these texts make clear that the growth of the church in Paul's mind is not a matter of recruits being added to the community (he had other words for that), but of the community being fitted for its destiny through the transforming power of Spirit-taught truth.

Paul's Word-and-Spirit perspective with regard to the church's destiny appears also in his parting speech to the Ephesian elders, as Luke records it in Acts 20:17-35. A glance at this passage will confirm what we have been saying.

Paul speaks first of his ministry of the Word. "I have declared to both Jews and Greeks that they must turn to God in repentance and have faith in our Lord Jesus" (verse 21). "I have gone about preaching the kingdom" (verse 25). "I have not hesitated to proclaim to you the whole will (purpose, NRSV) of God" (verse 27). He then speaks of the church, and does so in a way which shows that for him the church is central in God's purpose. It is "the church of God, which he bought with his own blood" (verse 28); it is God's flock, threatened by wolves (teachers of error), and needing therefore the maximum of watchful fidelity from its stated guardians. He refers, strikingly, to the Holy Spirit as having made the elders "overseers" to shepherd the church (verse 28); what he means is that the Holy Spirit himself oversaw the process of their selection and appointment, and the implication is that if they now seek his help for discharging their responsibilities they will receive it. And he concludes: "Now I commit you to God and to *the word of his grace, which can build you up* and give you an inheritance among all those who are sanctified" (verse 32).

"Build up" (or, simply, "build": there is no "up" in the Greek) is the same word as in Matthew 16:18, and here too, as indeed throughout the New Testament, it has a corporate frame of reference. "I will build *my church*," says Jesus; and "the word of his grace . . . can build you up and give you *an inheritance among all those who are sanctified*," says Paul. The building up of individuals is the winding down of individualism, for it is precisely the building of them into the communal network called the church. The Word, ministered, memorized, and masticated by meditation, has power to do the building up ("exercise of power" is the force of the Greek for "can" in verse 32) through the agency of the Holy Spirit. And within the church on earth this process of building up—or building in, as we might equally well call it when we focus on the people who are its object—goes on all the time. Jesus builds his church, according to his Word.

THE OLD TESTAMENT CHURCH

Now arises a question that Bible students often ask. Jesus spoke of his church-building work as future: "I will build . . ." All the New Testament teaching about the church centers on Christ—his coming, dying, rising, ascending to the throne, and pouring out the Spirit. Did the church that the incarnate Son of God is currently building start, then, through his historical ministry, or was God building a church in the manner described in Old Testament times? The answer is both yes and no, depending on the angle from which the question is put.

If your perspective is strictly historical—if, that is, you are asking about the appearance on earth of a community acknowledging Jesus as the Christ, then the question answers itself: obviously there could be no community of Christ's followers till Christ was there to be followed, nor could the full blessing of Pentecost be enjoyed till the Pentecostal outpouring of the Holy Spirit had taken place. The New Testament church is the church of Christ and of the Spirit; so, historically speaking, the often-heard statement that the church began at Pentecost has to be true.

If, however, your perspective is theological as well as historical—if, that is, you are asking about God's relationship to different individuals and groups at different times—the answer to the question then has more in it than has just been stated, and it becomes clear as the relevant data are reviewed that it is more misleading to deny the reality of an Old Testament church than to affirm it.

The New Testament writers teach us to read the Old Testament as a historical witness to a preparatory era in which under God everything was working up to the coming of the Messiah, who would establish the new order of God's kingdom in this disordered world. But throughout this era, right from the start, God was making known the gracious King-and-subjects covenant whereby he says to humans, "I, your maker, am your God to lead and guide you; you are my people, and each of you is my person, to honor and serve me." God's relationship with Adam and Eve in Eden was covenantal in this sense, and when God continued to maintain the relationship and to draw people into acceptance of it despite their fallenness, it stood revealed in practice as a covenant of grace. "I, your maker *against whom you have sinned*, nonetheless declare myself your God . . ." "Your God" means God who cares for you and is engaged to bless you up to the limit of his sovereign abilities—in other words, in a quite unlimited way. Within the covenant, as the King-and-subjects dimension suggests, there is disciplinary deprivation and chastening for unfaithfulness; yet the relationship itself is meant for blessing and enrichment.

It is truly said that biblical religion is covenant religion, in the Old Testament no less than in the New, and that in both Testaments true religion—covenant religion—is a matter of personal pronouns: namely, of humans being able to say "*my* God" in the knowledge that God says of and to each of them, "*my* person—*my* servant—*my* child—*my* covenant partner." Each "my" here is covenant language. It is also truly said that the New Testament church is God's covenant community, which makes it at least natural to speak of God's covenant community in Old Testament times as the church before Christ. But in saying this we run ahead of ourselves; we need for a moment to backtrack.

Who is in covenant with God? Answer: those who actively accept the covenant relationship that he extends to them and live to him in covenantal responsiveness, which is faith in its broadest notion. Abel, Enoch, and Noah, along with Abraham, are among those of whom Hebrews 11:4-16 says that "God is not ashamed to be called *their* God" (covenant language, note!) because they lived to him in faith. Genesis 4:25-26 implies that Seth's whole line were covenanting people. Genesis 17 tells how God established his covenant formally with Abraham's family through Isaac—that is, as events proved, with Israel's twelve tribes. The books of Exodus through Deuteronomy detail the law-code that God gave his covenant people after rescuing them from Egypt. This code centers on the Ten Commandments, which are framed by the introductory declaration, "I am the LORD your God . . ." (covenant language again!) (Ex. 20:2; Dt. 5:6). God's laws are thus covenant legislation.

In every era only a minority of Israelites ever took covenant obedience seriously, while the rest, though under God's covenant nationally and nominally, were not in a covenanted relationship with him personally. But there were always some, a remnant, who lived, labored, and often suffered loss, in loyal faith, relying on God's promises, worshiping and praying, and practicing neighbor-love, covenantal morality according to the Law, and fellowship for mutual encouragement. Not to call this faithful remnant the Old Testament church, when its members related to God precisely as Christians relate to him and were constantly doing together precisely what the Christian community does, would be strange indeed.

It appears, then, that in the Old Testament we are confronted with two things together. One is the reality of true and false religion among the official covenant people, the community that we today would call the visible church. The difference here between now and then was partly one of knowledge and partly one of experience. The faithful in Old Testament times did not know as much about the Christ to whom they looked forward as New Testament Christians do now that Christ has come; nor did Old Testament saints experience so much of God's transforming moral power in their lives as Christians have known since the Pentecostal outpouring of the Spirit. But faith, repentance, temptation, love, doubt, unbelief, praise, prayer, pride, thanksgiving, backsliding, patience, purity of heart, self-control, zeal for God—in short, all virtues belonging to godliness, and all vices comprising irreligion, were essentially the same in Old Testament times as they are in the New, and the Old Testament contains profound teaching about them. At the same time (and this is the second thing we find), a great deal of the covenantal order that God established for Israel through Moses was typical and temporary; imposed by God for educational reasons till Christ should come, it now no longer applies to anyone. The New Testament tells us what belongs in this latter category, and the lesson is one that Christian readers of the Old Testament absolutely must learn.

TYPE AND ANTITYPE

To be specific, then: a *type* in Scripture (*tupos* in Greek, meaning originally a die-stamp or matching impression) is an event, institution, place, object, office, or functioning person that patterns a greater reality that in some sense is of the same kind and is due to appear on history's stage at some subsequent point. This greater reality is called the antitype. The term "type" is taken from Romans 5:14, where Adam is called a *tupos* ("pattern") of Christ, the one who was to come. "Antitype" comes from 1 Peter 3:21, where baptism, understood not simply as an applying of water to the body but also, and essentially, as an outgoing of faith to God, is called the *antitype* that the preserving of Noah through the flood waters by his entering the ark had prefigured.

A type establishes a frame for interpreting the greater reality when it appears, and meantime, simply by existing, it inculcates the principle of which the greater reality will in fact be the supreme instance. When the greater reality arrives, it becomes the decisive factor in its own field; one way or another it transcends and supersedes the type. In space-time terms, the type is thenceforth a thing of the past, no longer determinative of what must be done or of what will happen. The biblical account of it, however, is of permanent value as providing concepts and categories for understanding the antitype. Typology thus becomes a kind of phrase book for use in theology.

Many types appear in Scripture, but those that are important for interpreting the book of Nehemiah are three in number.

First: under the Mosaic dispensation of God's covenant, the dispensation that the letter to the Hebrews calls "the former" and "the first" and declares to be "obsolete" since Christ came (Heb. 7:18; 8:7, 13; 9:1), covenant fellowship with Israel's holy God was maintained in the face of Israel's constant sins through a typical system of sacrifices managed by a typical priesthood in a sanctuary that typified the immediate presence of God. Jesus Christ's priestly ministry and mediation, his once-for-all sacrifice and unceasing intercession, supersedes all this, as Hebrews 7–10 makes clear. In Nehemiah's day, however, the prescribed path to fellowship with God was the obedient offering of the set sacrifices, and without this God's favor could not be expected.

Second: under the old covenant Israel was given a land,

Palestine, with promises of prosperity and protection for faithfulness, warnings of impoverishment and expulsion for unfaithfulness, and hints that there could be restoration after chastening judgment should penitence prevail. The land was a type of "a better country—a heavenly one" (Heb. 11:16), a country that is to be defined not geographically but relationally, in terms of fellowship with Christ and his people and enjoyment of the good things he gives to those who trust and serve him. In Nehemiah's day, however, the land was the appointed place of blessing, the blessing that was promised centered upon freedom from want, and renewal of life among God's languishing people involved return to the land from exile and reclamation of the land from pagan control.

Third: under the old covenant Jerusalem, the city of David and of Solomon's temple, was recognized as the place where God had chosen "to put his Name . . . as a dwelling for his Name" (Dt. 12:21, 11)—that is, Israel's appointed worship center, where the sacrifices should be offered, the ceremonial worship kept up, and the presence of God be sought and enjoyed. Under the new covenant, we find that God's own people in Christ constitute his temple (Eph. 2:19-22), and his presence to bless may be enjoyed wherever his servants call on him through Christ, or call on Christ as God's vice-gerent (Heb. 4:15-16; 10:19-22), while "Jerusalem" and "Zion" have become names for a community that is not of this world (Gal. 4:26; Heb. 12:22; Rev. 3:12; 21:2, 10), a community that now stands revealed as the antitype of which earthly Jerusalem was the type. In Nehemiah's day, however, it was categorically necessary, because divinely prescribed, that God be worshiped in Jerusalem—which meant that Jerusalem needed to be in a condition in which it could honor him publicly as was his due.

THE BOOK OF NEHEMIAH

We are now equipped to tune in to the book of Nehemiah and understand what it is about.

It is one of a pair, for Ezra and Nehemiah clearly belong together; and it is one of a set, for Ezra and Nehemiah clearly constitute a follow-on from the books of Chronicles. The Chronicler reviews Israelite history from David to the exile with a focus on the temple and on the worship and the spiritual life of the kings, the priests, and the people. Ezra and Nehemiah maintain this focus. Nehemiah 1–7 and 13 read like extracts from Nehemiah's diary, and chapters 8–12 read like official records that Nehemiah wrote into his narrative when, perhaps as a retirement task (he was a politician, after all, whatever else he was), he prepared his memoirs for public view. Chapter 13 as it stands would lose much of its point if chapters 8–12 were not there, as we shall see.

The story Nehemiah tells is a fascinating one. It deals with the rebuilding of Jerusalem's walls (chs. 1–6), the renewing of Jerusalem's worship (chs. 8–10), the repopulating of Jerusalem's streets (chs. 11–12), and finally the renewing of Jerusalem's renewal, which over the years had gone lamentably off the boil (ch. 13). So it is at the same time the story of the literal building up of Jerusalem (the type), namely the city in Palestine, and the story of the spiritual building up of Jerusalem (the antitype), namely the covenant people of God, the Old Testament church. Nehemiah through God built walls; God through Nehemiah built saints. Humanly, Nehemiah is the key figure in both stories. His book reveals him as a pastoral leader *par excellence*, devoted and dynamic, humble, zealous, wise, and patient, and at every point, like Moses, Paul, Martin Luther, Oliver Cromwell and Winston Churchill, seeming a little larger than life by reason of the clarity with which he defined his goals and the energy with which he pursued them. From this standpoint, his book may be read as the record of a personal triumph of a pastoral and political sort. But equally it may be read as a witness to God's dealing with both Nehemiah and those he served in such a way as to work in them qualities of vitality, fidelity, bravery, tenacity, generosity, and maturity: qualities of godliness that God is constantly fostering in his church, and that from our vantage-point we recognize as Christlike. This is undoubtedly the right approach.

The book of Nehemiah, then, should be read as testimony to the renewing and sanctifying of the church. Nehemiah's motive in composing it is evidently doxological, not vainglorious; he is writing for the praise of God, not of himself; he is testifying to what God has done in and through him, not to anything he might claim as a personal achievement. "I glory in Christ Jesus in my service to God," wrote Paul five centuries later; "I will not venture to speak of anything except what Christ has accomplished through me in leading the Gentiles to obey God by what I have said and done" (Rom. 15:17-18). In just the same way, Nehemiah glories in God and what God has wrought through him for the spiritual welfare of others, and the aim of his book is to lead his readers to share his glorying with him.

It appears, then, that the way of wisdom in exploring the book of Nehemiah is to be equally interested both in how Nehemiah led the people and in how God led Nehemiah, and to keep the well-being of the church as the main focus of interest as we pursue these two inquiries. So this is what we shall try to do in the pages that follow.

CHAPTER ONE

Meet Nehemiah

I like him; he was a construction man," the old Texan housebuilder told me. I was glad to hear him say it, for, frankly, I like Nehemiah too, and I hope when I get to heaven I shall be able to meet him and tell him so. What I would like him to know is that during the half-century that I have been a Christian he has helped me enormously, more perhaps than any other Bible character apart from the Lord Jesus himself. When at nineteen I began to wonder if God wanted me in the professional ministry, it was Nehemiah's experience that showed me how vocational guidance is given and set me on the road to being sure. When I was put in charge of a study center committed to outflanking and defusing liberal theology, it was Nehemiah who gave me the clues I needed about leading enterprises for God and dealing with entrenched opposition. When after that I became principal of a theological college that was in low water, it was once again Nehemiah whose example of leadership showed me how to do my job. Since what you can see you can also say, when I have been asked to speak on vocation and/or leadership I have often taken my hearers on a trek through parts of Nehemiah's story. Naturally one has warm feelings towards those to whom one is indebted, and I am very deeply indebted to Nehemiah; no one should wonder, therefore, that now I regard him as a particular friend.

Nor am I the only one so to regard him. A book published in 1986 began like this:

> The details of my first meeting with him are hazy in my mind. God sent him to me during my early university years to help me overcome some formidable challenges. He has been a close companion ever since. . . .
>
> Nehemiah put his very being into his journal, which is incorporated into the book we now call by his name. As I read I can feel his heartbeats, sense the trembling of his fingers, know the heaviness of his groans. . . . What wisdom he had! And how he drummed the basic lessons of leadership into me! I have forgotten none of them and have gone back to him time and again for reassurance.
>
> As a medical student I had a special need of him. He was a leader. And so, whether I wanted to be or not, was I. . . . I became, in a relatively short time, the national chairman of British Inter-Varsity. . . . During this period Nehemiah comforted and instructed me. . . . I chose to expound the book of Nehemiah at the first Latin American Fellowship of Evangelical Students. . . . Nehemiah became a sort of patron saint of the new movement—or at least a guiding light to young student leaders facing the awesome task of evangelizing a continent. . . .
>
> As one responsibility replaced another, I continued to be fascinated and instructed by the life and words of this man of action. And as I grew older I gleaned more from him. It was the man, not the book, that held me. . . . He has become my model for leadership.[1]

When first I read these words of John White, I laughed out loud, as sometimes one cannot help doing in face of the delightful things that God does. John White and I are almost contemporaries and have several things in common (a British Inter-Varsity nurture; British genes tied to Canadian citizenship; an evangelical theology, a pastoral constraint, and a call to authorship; plus homes in the Lower Mainland of British Columbia). But not till 1986 did I know that we shared a parallel relationship with Nehemiah. The paragraphs quoted, however, take words right out of my heart. I wonder how many more there are who have been mentored by Nehemiah in this way.

NEHEMIAH'S FLAWS

Yet Nehemiah does not appear in everyone's list of favorite Bible characters, and that, I guess, is for at least two reasons. To start with, many Christians know very little about him. Their Old Testament reading is sketchy at best, and the book of Nehemiah is one that they never go near. Knowing that Nehemiah is not mentioned in the New Testament, they infer that he is not important, and so take no interest in him. If they were told how strong is the case for bracketing him with Moses, as the re-founder under God of the nation that God used Moses to create, they would be surprised.

Moreover, some of those who know something about him have formed an unappealing image of him that keeps them from taking him seriously as a man of God. They see him as a rather savage person who habitually threw his weight about and would never have been pleasant company under any circumstances at all. They note the imprecations in his prayers—"Give them over as plunder in a land of captivity. Do not cover up their guilt or blot out their sins from your sight" (Neh. 4:4-5; compare 6:14 and 13:29, where "remember" means "remember for judgment"). They observe that on at least one occasion he cursed and beat some of his compatriots and pulled out their hair (13:25). They conclude that he was hardly a good man; certainly not a man of great spiritual stature, from whom precious lessons can be learned.

What is the appropriate comment on such an estimate? First, there was indeed a rough edge to Nehemiah; there is to most leaders. In terms of the classic four temperaments, he appears to have been a choleric, a robust, restless, forthright man who was happiest when plowing energy into a challenging project and who found it easier (as we say nowadays) to *do* than to *be*. People of that sort are often found frightening, particularly when their zeal leads them, as sometimes it does, to speak and act in a way that is excessively emphatic. But, second, horses for courses; God had prepared Nehemiah for a task that a less forthright man could not have done. And, third, Jesus' cleansing of the temple and denouncing of the Pharisees was rougher than anything recorded of Nehemiah; if we think that Jesus' violence was justified, we should grant the possibility that Nehemiah's was too. I shall say more about this in the appropriate place.

I do not, however, contend that Nehemiah was sinless. I should be foolish to the point of blasphemy if I did. Jesus Christ is the only sinless person whom we meet in the Bible story; he is the only sinless person there ever was. All the rest of God's servants have been fallen creatures, sinners saved by grace, and sometimes their sinfulness shows. Whether Nehemiah had red hair I do not know, but he certainly had a red-headed intensity about him that expressed itself in a somewhat un-Christlike ferocity of style. This was the defect of his quality, the limitation that went with his strength. Every servant of God fails one way or another to be flawless, and Nehemiah was no exception to that rule. Yet his strengths were marvelous; so I hope that no one will lose interest in him simply because we have agreed that he was not perfect.

NEHEMIAH'S STRENGTHS

What special strengths do we see in Nehemiah? Three, at least. First, he is a model of *personal zeal*—zeal, that is, for the honor and glory of God. As he says in one of his prayers, he is one of those "who delight in revering your name" (1:11), and the strength of his passion to magnify the Lord is very great. Such zeal, though matched by Jesus and the psalmists and Paul (to look no further), is rarer today than it should be; most of us are more like the lukewarm Laodiceans, drifting along very cheerfully in becalmed churches, feeling confident that everything is all right, and thereby disgusting our Lord Jesus, who sees that, spiritually speaking, nothing is right (see Rev. 3:14-22). The rough language of our Lord's threat to spit out the Laodicean church—that is, to repudiate and reject it—shows that zeal for God's house still constrains him in his glory, just as it did on earth when he cleansed the temple (Jn. 2:17). Back in the days when God used his own people as his executioners, not only in holy war with pagans but also in the disciplining of the church, Phinehas the priest had speared an Israelite and his Midianite whore together, and God through Moses had commended him for a zeal that matched God's own: "he was as zealous as I am for my honor among them . . . tell him I am making my covenant of peace with him . . . because he was zealous for the honor of his God" (Num. 25:11-13). As God himself is zealous, so must his servants be.

Are we clear what zeal is? It is not fanaticism; it is not wildness; it is not irresponsible enthusiasm; it is not any form of pushy egoism. It is, rather, a humble, reverent, businesslike, single-minded commitment to the hallowing of God's name and the doing of his will.

> A zealous man in religion is pre-eminently a man of
> one thing. It is not enough to say that he is earnest,

hearty, uncompromising, thorough-going, whole-hearted, fervent in spirit. He only sees one thing, he cares for one thing, he lives for one thing, he is swallowed up in one thing; and that one thing is to please God. Whether he lives, or whether he dies—whether he has health, or whether he has sickness—whether he is rich, or whether he is poor—whether he pleases men, or whether he gives offence—whether he is thought wise, or whether he is thought foolish—whether he gets honour, or whether he gets shame—for all this the zealous man cares nothing at all. He burns for one thing; and that one thing is, to please God, and to advance God's glory.[2]

Zealous folk are sensitive to situations in which God's truth and honor are in one way or another being jeopardized, and rather than let the matter go by default they will force the issue on people's attention in order to compel if possible a change of heart about it—even at personal risk. Nehemiah was zealous in this sense, as we shall see, and his zeal is an example to us all.

The second strength that we find in Nehemiah is *pastoral commitment*: the commitment of a leader, a natural mover and shaker, to compassionate service for the needy. A leader is a person who can persuade others to embrace and pursue his or her own purpose; as (I think) Harry Truman once expressed it, the leader's business is to get other people to do what they do not want to do and to make them like doing it. One is only a leader if one is actually followed, just as one is only a teacher if others actually learn from one; so to be a leader, one has to be able to motivate others. But then one is in danger of becoming a dictator, using one's persuasive power to manipulate and exploit those whom one leads. Nehemiah, however, was not like that. He was no more a dictator than he was a doormat; he did not ride roughshod over people any more than he allowed people to ride roughshod over him. As he expressed love for God by his concentrated zeal, so he expressed love for neighbor by his compassionate care. He consciously shouldered responsibility for others' well-being: he saw the restoring of Jerusalem as a welfare operation, no less than an honoring of God, and he took time out at least once from the building of the walls to help the poor (see 5:1-13), in addition to permanently forgoing his right to claim support from those he governed (5:14-18).

Nehemiah slips a number of his prayers into his memoirs, and some of these have generated puzzlement. "Remember me with favor, O my God, for all I have done for these people" (5:19, following the account of his social service) is a case in point. More such "remember me" prayers appear in 13:14, 22, 31. What goes on here? we ask. Is Nehemiah aiming to build up a merit balance in God's ledger? Is he asking to be justified by his works? Not at all. He refers to what he has done simply as a token of his integrity and sincerity in ministry, a proof of his genuineness as a servant of the servants of God—in other words, as evidence of his living out the pastoral commitment of which I have been speaking.

The third strength that Nehemiah displays is *practical wisdom*, the ability to make realistic plans and get things done. From this standpoint, Nehemiah's memoirs constitute a crash course in managerial skills. Once he has succeeded in exchanging his comfortable life as a high-level palace lackey (royal cupbearer) for the problematical role of governor of Judah, with malcontents constantly yapping at his heels as he seeks to rebuild and reorganize Jerusalem, we see him rising to the challenge of every situation with truly masterful insight and ingenuity. We watch him securing a safe-conduct and chits for building materials from the king; organizing and overseeing the building of the wall; arranging Jerusalem's defenses while the building went on; defusing discontent and averting a threatened strike within the work force; maintaining morale till the job was done; conducting tricky negotiations with both friend and foe; and finally imposing and reimposing unappreciated rules about race, temple services, and Sabbath observance. Nehemiah's headaches as top man were many, and the sanctified versatility with which he handles all these things is wonderful to watch.

And his achievements were as outstanding as his gifts. He rebuilt the ruined wall of Jerusalem in fifty-two days, when nobody else thought it could be rebuilt at all. He restored regular temple worship, regular instruction from God's Law, serious Sabbath keeping, and godly family life. He was the true re-founder of Israel's corporate life after the exile, following the relative failure to restore it during the previous hundred years. He takes his place, by right, as it seems to me, with the greatest leaders of God's people in the Bible story—with Moses and David and Paul. Nehemiah was a truly marvelous man.

Yet Nehemiah himself would be the first to rebuke me if I left the matter there, for he knew, and insists in his book, that what he accomplished was no mere human achievement and would be misunderstood if it were treated as such. The prayers for help with which he punctuates his story show where he believed that his strength lay, and where on a day-to-day basis he looked for support (see 1:4-11; 2:4; 4:4, 9; 6:9). His references to what God "put in [his] heart" (2:12; 7:5) show where he thought his vision and wisdom came from. And his statement "the wall was completed . . . in fifty-two days . . . our enemies . . . realized that this work had been done *with the help of our God*" (6:15-16) really says it all. "Don't give me the credit," protests Nehemiah in effect; "what is done through human agents like me is done by God, and he must have the praise for it." I agree, and I hope my readers do too. *Soli Deo Gloria* (to God alone be glory)!

NEHEMIAH'S GOD

What makes a man of God is first and foremost his vision of God, and it will help us to know Nehemiah better if at this point we look at his beliefs about God, as his book reveals them. I assume, as must by now be obvious, the unity of the book as a product of Nehemiah's own mind. We have already seen that its core is the personal memoirs of this man of action (chapters 1–7 and 13), to which has been added what reads like an official record of the inaugural exercises of worship in restored Jerusalem (chapters 8–12). The list of builders in chapter 3, the census list of chapter 7, the signatories list in 10:1-27, and the lists of residents in and around Jerusalem, with priests and Levites, that fill chapters 11:3–12:26 are the kind of material that nowadays would be put in appendices; but the ancient way was simply to incorporate everything in the text. The natural guess is that, like a modern politician who suspects, or hopes, that he belongs in future history books, Nehemiah devoted some part of his retirement to composing what is in effect his political testament and personal testimony rolled into one; and to this end he drew on the journal he had kept during his years as a public figure, plus official sources to which, as an ex-governor of Judah, he had direct access.

Ezra's book, on this view, would naturally then have been written as a companion volume, to link Nehemiah's achievement with what had preceded since the end of the exile.

However that may be—and none of it, I grant, can be proved for certain—Nehemiah's book is a unity, and we are not therefore wrong to proceed on the basis that by writing chapters 8–12 into his text Nehemiah endorsed and made his own all that they declare about God and his ways, even if he did not originally draft them.

What Nehemiah gives us from his journal tells us, as

Matthew Henry the Puritan put it, not only about the works of his hands but also about the workings of his heart; in fact, it tells us almost more about the latter than about the former. But the workings of Nehemiah's heart in faith and prayer and hope and confidence and acceptance of sanctified risk and waging spiritual war against what we can recognize as demonically-driven discouragements and distractions all express and reflect his knowledge of God. And this began for him, as it must for everyone, with knowledge *about* God: the conceptual knowledge that we call theology. Theology, meaning truths about God in the mind, is not the same thing as a relationship with God, as the orthodoxy of the devils demonstrates (see Jas. 2:19). But without true theology, though there may be a strong sense of God's reality (as in Hinduism and animism and the New Age), entry into the covenant bond whereby we know that God is truly and eternally ours is not possible. So, if we want to come close to Nehemiah and enrich our relationship with God from his, we must get a grip on his theology.

Some years ago I played hooky for two evenings from a theological conference in New York that was boring me stiff. On one of the evenings a fellow refugee took me to a jazz club, and I spent the other at the Metropolitan Opera, where Wagner's *Tannhäuser* was being performed. During the first intermission a youngish lady sitting next to me started chatting with me about the production, and as opera buffs do we became quite animated. It seemed that her husband, sitting on the other side of her, was not an opera man and felt excluded. I became aware that he was glaring at me and had clamped his hand firmly on the lady's knee—I suppose as a sign of ownership. Then he whisked her abruptly away, to sit elsewhere for the rest of the performance. It was embarrassing. Maybe he thought I was getting fresh. Maybe his wife had started too many conversations with other men in the past. Maybe he had been dragged to the opera against his will and wanted to work a bit of mad off on someone. At all events, he was evidently feeling at that moment that his wife was closer to me than she was to him, and he did not like it. And—this is the point—what he felt was in one sense right, for she and I knew a bit about opera, and lacking that knowledge he could not comprehend what we were sharing, nor share it with us. In the same way, unless we know what Nehemiah knew about God we shall not be able to comprehend and share the vision and the passion that propelled him through his years of ministry and made him such a shining example to us of servant leadership.

So we ask: what did Nehemiah believe about the one whom ten times over, six times in transcribed prayers, he calls "my God"? What did Nehemiah's faith in God amount to? The answer is clear from the book itself.

In the first place, the God of Nehemiah is the transcendent Creator, the God "of heaven" (1:4-5; 2:4, 20), self-sustaining, self-energizing, and eternal ("from everlasting to everlasting," 9:5). He is "great" (8:6), "great and awesome" (1:5; 4:14), "great, mighty and awesome" (9:32), and the angels ("the multitudes of heaven") worship him (9:6). Lord of history, God of judgment and mercy, "a forgiving God, gracious and compassionate, slow to anger and abounding in love" (9:17; see Ex. 34:6-7), God was to Nehemiah the sublimest, most permanent, most pervasive, most intimate, most humbling, exalting, and commanding of all realities. The basis on which, like William Carey the missionary, Nehemiah attempted great things for God and expected great things from God was that, like the Calvinist Carey, he had grasped the greatness of God himself.

In the second place, the God of Nehemiah is Yahweh, "the LORD," the covenant-making, covenant-keeping, promise-fulfilling, faithful God of Israel (9:8, 32, 33). The prayer out of which Nehemiah's ministry was born began, "O LORD, God of heaven, the great and awesome God, *who keeps his covenant of love* . . ." and goes on to beg that God will bless "*your* servants and *your* people, *whom you redeemed* [from Egypt, long ago]" (1:5, 10; cf. 9:9-25). The personal pronouns in the phrases "*your* people," "*our* God" (4:4, 20; 6:16; 10:32, 34, 36, 37, 38, 39; 13:2, 18, 27), and "*my* God" (2:8, 12, 18; 5:19; 6:14; 7:5; 13:14, 22, 29, 31) are affirmations of the covenant relationship between God and Israelites as an established fact, and invocations of it as a basis for trust and hope and obedience. God's covenant, like the marriage covenant, was a mutual bond of both possession and self-giving: God possessed Israel as his people and gave himself to them to bless them by his gifts and guidance, while the Israelites possessed Yahweh as their God and professed themselves given to him to honor him by their worship and service. The prayerful dependence on God that sustained Nehemiah throughout his leadership career, and that he so often verbalizes as his book goes along, was an expression of his faith in God's covenantal commitment to him and to those he led, just as was his declaration as he arranged Jerusalem's defenses, "Our God will fight for us!" (4:20). Nor was his faith in God's faithfulness disappointed. Nehemiah's God showed himself to be a faithful covenanter who did not let his servant down.

In the third place, the God of Nehemiah is a God whose words of revelation are true and trustworthy. By means of Spirit-taught instruction given through Moses and the prophets (1:8; 8:1, 14; 9:13, 30; cf. 9:20), God had told his people who he was, what he wanted from them, how he would react should they rebel, and what he would do should they come to their senses and repent after rebelling. "Remember," prayed Nehemiah, "the instruction you gave your servant Moses, saying, 'If you are unfaithful, I will scatter you among the nations, but if you return to me and obey my commands, then even if your exiled people are at the farthest horizon, I will gather them from there and bring them to the place I have chosen as a dwelling for my Name'" (1:8, alluding to Lev. 26, especially verse 33; Dt. 28:64 and 30:1-10, especially verse 4). Here, at the outset of his book, we see Nehemiah dealing with God on the basis that he is the God who stands by what he has said.

Later, Ezra (Neh. 8:1-6) and Nehemiah (8:9-10) treated the time given to reading, preaching, and teaching God's Law as a great national occasion, precisely because what God had set out in the books of Moses as his will for Israel was still in force. That was why it was so important that ignorance of the Law be banished, and then that past sins of disregard for the Law be solemnly confessed and renounced, and then that a new commitment "to obey carefully all the commands, regulations and decrees of the LORD our Lord" (10:29) be made (see chapters 9–10). The Law that God gave his covenant people to show them how to please him was, for Nehemiah, the unchanging standard of righteousness, just as God's promises were, for him, the unchanging basis of future hope and present confidence. Nehemiah thus comes to model for us, in Old Testament terms, what it means to live by the conviction expressed in the old Christian song:

> *Trust and obey,*
> *For there's no other way*
> *To be happy in Jesus*
> *Than to trust and obey.*

These three convictions about God were most certainly the making of Nehemiah. Without them, he would never have cared enough about God's honor in Jerusalem to pray that the city be restored, nor would he have sought the taxing and terrifying role of being the leader in that restoration, nor would he have had what it took to keep going in face of all the apathy and animosity that his leadership encoun-

tered. While it is clear that by temperament he was masterful to the point of being autocratic and tough to the point of
stubbornness, these qualities alone would never have
brought forth the patience, goodwill, sense of responsibility, and freedom from defensive cynicism that marked him
throughout. The quality in Nehemiah that C. S. Lewis
called obstinacy in belief, the keeping-on-keeping-on factor,
had about it something supernatural that can only be
explained in the way that the writer to the Hebrews explains
Moses' steadiness in challenging the king of Egypt and leading out the Israelite rabble on pilgrimage to their new
land—"he persevered because he saw him who is invisible"
(Heb. 11:27). It is only those who "see" the great, mighty,
gracious, faithful covenant God of the Bible who are able to
endure the kind of pressures that Moses and Nehemiah
faced—pressures involving extremes of what England's
slang of the seventies called "aggro"—and hence real risk to
life and limb. This vision breeds hope, raises morale, and
sustains commitment in a way that is beyond the understanding either of the world or of those in the church whose
view of God has shrunk.

It has been computed that the various lapses of the twentieth century into political, tribal, and sociological bar-
barisms have produced more martyrdoms than any previous
century saw, even the second and third, during which
Christianity was a prohibited religion and official persecu-
tions broke out again and again. And it is simply a matter of
fact that those who have given up their lives rather than give
up their faith have come from those Christian circles in
which this biblical vision of the living God has been taught
and upheld.

For the best part of two centuries, forms of the intellectual chameleon called liberalism, or modernity, have domi-
nated the mainline churches of the West. The taproot of
modernist liberalism is the idea, issuing from the so-called

Enlightenment, that the world has the wisdom, so that the Christian way must always be to absorb and adjust to what the world happens to be saying at the moment about human life. *Deism*, which banishes God entirely from the world of human affairs, and the view nowadays called *panentheism* or *monism*, which imprisons him pervasively but impotently within it, have been the two poles between which liberal thinking about God has swung. But neither of these God-concepts is, or can be, trinitarian; neither has room for any belief in the incarnation, or in an objective atonement, or in an empty tomb, or in the sovereign cosmic Lordship of the living Christ today; and neither squares with the affirmation that biblical teaching is divinely revealed truth. It is no wonder, then, that liberalism typically produces, not martyrs, nor challengers of the secular status quo, but trimmers, people who are always finding reasons for going along with the cultural consensus of the moment, whether on abortion, sexual permissiveness, the basic identity of all religions, the impropriety of evangelism and missionary work, or anything else.

In the last century, when ideas of progress were in the air and it was possible to believe that every day in every way the world was getting better and better, liberalism, which presented itself as progressive Christianity, could be made to appear right-minded; in our day, however, thinking people are bound to find it wrong-headed. Today, after all the horrors our era has seen, the idea that the world is the repository of wisdom seems no better than a bad joke, and the view that rates the Christianity of our fathers, the Christianity that produced Augustine and Luther and Whitefield and Wesley and Spurgeon and Lloyd-Jones and Billy Graham, as a ragbag of outmoded crudities on which we can improve looks like the nonsense that it really is. The only sort of Christianity that can reasonably claim attention for the future is the Bible-based Christianity that defines God in scriptural terms and offers, not affirmation, but transformation of our disordered lives.

One hopeful sign amid the large-scale confusion that marks the modern church is that more and more of those who profess to be Christians are receiving the Bible as the Word of God and taking the God whom we meet in its pages with full seriousness, just as did the Reformers and the Puritans and the evangelical awakeners of the eighteenth century. It has been like that wherever at any time in history the Spirit of God has moved in revival. It was so in Nehemiah's day, as we shall see, and it is still the case that spiritual life starts again when starving souls turn, or return, to the Bible and its God. Perhaps God has not finally abandoned us, after all.

NEHEMIAH'S GODLINESS

People who live close to God are more God-conscious than self-conscious, and if you call them godly to their face they are likely to smile, shake their heads, and say how they wish it was true. What they know about themselves has more to do with their weaknesses and sins than with any real or fancied spiritual attainments, and they are reluctant to talk about themselves save as tools in God's hands, servants whose story only merits notice because it is part of the greater story of how God has exalted himself in this world that denies him honor. Nehemiah seems to have been that sort of saint, and the glimpses he gives us of his inner life are rare. By natural makeup he was as obviously an extrovert as Jeremiah was an introvert, and it is in any case the way of extroverts to focus on matters outside themselves. Three things at least, however, can be specified with certainty about his spiritual life, in each of which he is a shining example to Christian believers.

First, Nehemiah's walk with God was *saturated with his*

praying, and praying of the truest and purest kind—namely, the sort of praying that is always seeking to clarify its own vision of who and what God is, and to celebrate his reality in constant adoration, and to rethink in his presence such needs and requests as one is bringing to him, so that the stating of them becomes a specifying of "hallowed be thy name . . . thy will be done . . . for thine is the kingdom, the power, and the glory." As we began to see earlier, Nehemiah punctuates his story with prayers to "my God," who is "our God." He starts his book with a full transcript of his plea for the covenant people (1:5-11), he ends it with four "remember me" petitions, the last of which is actually his sign-off line (13:14, 22, 29, 30), and he goes out of his way to record several other prayers in the course of his narrative. (Did he write out these prayers at the time of first making them? It looks like it, and certainly countless praying people have found this a helpful thing to do.) It is clear that as a writer he understands, and now wants his readers to understand, that only ventures that are begun in prayer and bathed in prayer throughout are likely to be blessed as the venture of rebuilding Jerusalem's walls was blessed, and he so selects and arranges his material as to project this truth without having to put it into words. He tells us of his praying in order to teach us from his own example that it is prayer that changes things, and that without praying there is no prospering. Evidently he had learned this in the years before his book opens, so that when the bad news came from Jerusalem he knew that his first task was, as the old hymn says, to "carry everything to God in prayer."

Nehemiah's public life was the outflow, and thus the revelation, of his personal life, and his personal life as his narrative shows it to us was steeped in, and shaped by, habitual petitionary prayer, in which devotion to God, dependence on God, and desire for the glory of God found equal expression. In this he stands before us as a model. "Pray continually," "pray in the Spirit on all occasions," says Paul (1 Thess. 5:17; Eph. 6:18). Jesus told his disciples the parable of the unjust judge "to show them that they should always pray and not give up" (Lk. 18:1). Nehemiah's life teaches the same lesson. Constant private conversation with God, asking and adoring, is both a natural expression of a regenerate heart and a needful discipline for a spiritual leader, and Nehemiah's example at this point should be etched indelibly on all our minds.

Second, Nehemiah's walk with God involved *solidarity with his people*—the Jews, God's people—in their sin and need. He was a man of great gifts and marked individuality, earning his living in official Persian employment, first as royal cupbearer, then as provincial governor; this necessarily set him at a distance from other Jews outwardly, and could have cooled his passion for Jewish welfare inwardly as the years went by. But in fact his commitment to see Jerusalem built up, both materially and spiritually, never flagged. His zeal for this cause runs right through his book, becoming clear in its first sentences. The travelers from Jerusalem arrive, and Nehemiah asks them how the city is faring (1:1-2). They tell him that the walls are down again, the gates have been burned to the ground, and the scene is one of "great trouble and disgrace" for the returned community.

Hearing this, Nehemiah spends his off-duty hours for several days mourning, fasting, weeping, and praying—seeking, apparently, that God should show him what to pray for specifically (a constantly necessary step, be it said, in the practice of intercession) (1:3-4). "Then," with his mind clear at last and his petition formed and focused, he presents to God the plea that the Spirit of God has helped him put in order (1:5-11). And in this plea his expression of solidarity with the Jerusalem Jews is unqualified and complete. "I confess the sins we Israelites, including myself and my father's house, have

committed against you. We have acted very wickedly towards
you. We have not obeyed the commands, decrees and laws you
gave your servant Moses" (1:6-7). He acknowledges solidarity (*we*, not just *they*) because he knows that is how God sees
it. So he accepts a share in the shame of the people now under
judgment, and in this, too, he is a model for us.

Solidarity as communal involvement according to the
Scriptures—the solidarity of the family, the nation, and the
church—is something that we today do not understand very
well. Western culture teaches us to treat ourselves as isolated
individuals and to excuse ourselves from accepting solidarity
with any group, especially when the solidarity is one of disre-
pute. John White tells a quaint story to illustrate our attitude.

> As a medical student I once missed a practical class on
> venereal disease. Because of this I had to go to the vene-
> real diseases clinic alone one night at a time when stu-
> dents did not usually attend. As I entered the building,
> a male nurse I did not know met me. A line of men were
> waiting for treatment. "I want to see the doctor," I said.
>
> "That's what everybody wants. Stand in the line," he
> replied.
>
> "But you don't understand. I'm a medical student,"
> I protested.
>
> "Makes no difference. You got it the same way every-
> body else did. Stand in the line," the male nurse
> repeated.
>
> In the end I managed to explain to him why I was
> there, but I can still feel the sense of shame that made
> me balk at standing in line with men who had VD."[3]

Nehemiah, however, knew that God saw the Jews,
Abraham's seed, as one family, with a corporate responsibility and a corporate destiny, and he unhesitatingly identified
with them in the guilt that had brought them under judgment. Jesus behaved similarly when, as Saviour, he stood in

the line with sinners to undergo John's baptism of repentance; and so in the church must we. We have all had a greater share in the church's shortcomings and unfaithfulnesses than we know, and we may not therefore treat such sense as we have of its failures as excusing us from the need to confess that we shared in the process of its failing. Nor is it for us to turn our back on the church in impatience, as "parachurch" workers, so-called, sometimes do, but to pray and work for its renewal, keeping that as the prime focus of our concern at all times. This is a major lesson to be learned from our meeting with Nehemiah.

Third, Nehemiah's walk with God brought *sobriety about his powers*. This is a character trait that betokens real humility and maturity before God. Being humble is not a matter of pretending to be worthless, but is a form of realism, not only regarding the real badness of one's sins and stupidities and the real depth of one's dependence on God's grace, but also regarding the real range of one's abilities. Humble believers know what they can and cannot do. They note both their gifts and their limitations, and so are able to avoid both the unfaithfulness of letting their God-given powers lie fallow and the foolhardiness of biting off more than they can chew. Nehemiah had leadership and management gifts that he used up to the limit. His visionary practicality was a marvelous endowment, producing marvelous results. The way he motivated and directed the building of Jerusalem's walls, the repopulating of the city, and the reorganizing of temple supplies was truly Napoleonic. But when the agenda was the teaching of the Law and the first public gestures of renewed obedience to God, Nehemiah stood back and gave Ezra and the Levites the leadership role, intervening only at a moment of general confusion to urge the people to celebrate rather than weep (8:9-10). Otherwise, he limited himself to organizing the processions at the dedication of the wall (12:31, 38, 40). He knew he was not called or qualified to preach and teach, and he did not try to usurp these functions. In this he showed himself both humble and mature and revealed a realism about gifts and responsibilities that we shall do well to covet for ourselves.

Here, then, are three fundamental lessons for us to learn from Nehemiah's service of God before we move on to study the forms that his service took.

CHAPTER TWO

Called to Serve

The words of Nehemiah son of Hacaliah:

In the month of Kislev in the twentieth year, while I was in the citadel of Susa, Hanani, one of my brothers, came from Judah with some other men, and I questioned them about the Jewish remnant that survived the exile, and also about Jerusalem.

They said to me, "Those who survived the exile and are back in the province are in great trouble and disgrace. The wall of Jerusalem is broken down, and its gates have been burned with fire."

When I heard these things, I sat down and wept. For some days I mourned and fasted and prayed before the God of heaven. Then I said:

"O Lord, God of heaven, the great and awesome God, who keeps his covenant of love with those who love him and obey his commands, let your ear be attentive and your eyes open to hear the prayer your servant is praying before you day and night for your servants, the people of Israel. I confess the sins we Israelites, including myself and my father's house, have committed against you. We have acted very wickedly toward you. We have not obeyed the

commands, decrees and laws you gave your servant
Moses.

"Remember the instruction you gave your servant
Moses, saying, 'If you are unfaithful, I will scatter you
among the nations, but if you return to me and obey my
commands, then even if your exiled people are at the far-
thest horizon, I will gather them from there and bring
them to the place I have chosen as a dwelling for my
Name.'

"They are your servants and your people, whom you
redeemed by your great strength and your mighty hand.

"O Lord, let your ear be attentive to the prayer of this
your servant and to the prayer of your servants who
delight in revering your name. Give your servant success
today by granting him favor in the presence of this man."

I was cupbearer to the king.

In the month of Nisan in the twentieth year of King
Artaxerxes, when wine was brought for him, I took the
wine and gave it to the king. I had not been sad in his
presence before; so the king asked me, "Why does your
face look so sad when you are not ill? This can be nothing but sadness of heart."

I was very much afraid, but I said to the king, "May
the king live forever! Why should my face not look sad
when the city where my fathers are buried lies in ruins,
and its gates have been destroyed by fire?"

The king said to me, "What is it you want?"

Then I prayed to the God of heaven, and I
answered the king, "If it pleases the king and if your
servant has found favor in his sight, let him send me
to the city in Judah where my fathers are buried so
that I can rebuild it."

Then the king, with the queen sitting beside him,
asked me, "How long will your journey take, and
when will you get back?" It pleased the king to send
me; so I set a time.

I also said to him, "If it pleases the king, may I have

letters to the governors of Trans-Euphrates, so that
they will provide me safe-conduct until I arrive in
Judah? And may I have a letter to Asaph, keeper of the
king's forest, so he will give me timber to make beams
for the gates of the citadel by the temple and for the city
wall and for the residence I will occupy?" And because
the gracious hand of my God was upon me, the king
granted my requests.

(Nehemiah 1:1–2:8)

Now we move closer to Nehemiah's story of how God
led him to become Jerusalem's rebuilder. This is a classic
example of how God directs his servants, today as yesterday,
into the ministry tasks that he has in mind for them. We
noted earlier that some aspects of the New Testament order
of things stand in contrast to their Old Testament
antecedents, but here there is only continuity. God's current
way of making us aware of what roles he wants us to fulfill
in his kingdom is essentially the same as that we see in
Nehemiah's narrative. It is appropriate, therefore, to intro-
duce the story by establishing the Christian frame into
which we should fit it as we read it today.

A TWOFOLD CALL

The New Testament teaches that every Christian has a
twofold calling. First, God calls each of us individually to
believe and to serve. This first calling, so named because the
gospel invitation to turn from sin and trust Christ for eternal life is at its heart, is actually a work of power whereby
God brings us to faith through the Holy Spirit's action in
illuminating us through the gospel and moving us to
response. Chapter X of the Westminster Confession, titled
"Of Effectual Calling," focuses on this divine action very
comprehensively:

> All those whom God has predestined unto life . . . he is pleased . . . effectually to call, by his Word and Spirit, out of that state of sin and death, in which they are by nature, to grace and salvation by Jesus Christ; enlightening their minds spiritually and savingly to understand the things of God, taking away their heart of stone, and giving unto them an heart of flesh, renewing their wills and, by his almighty power, determining them to that which is good, and effectually drawing them to Jesus Christ: yet so, as they come most freely, being made willing by his grace.[1]

When Paul addresses the Roman Christians as those "called to belong to Jesus Christ . . . called to be saints" (Rom. 1:6-7; cf. 8:28; 1 Cor. 1:2), it is to this work of God that he is referring, and he regularly uses the verb "call" with God as subject to mean "bring to faith" (see Rom. 8:30; 1 Cor. 1:9, 26; 7:20, 24; Gal. 1:6, 15; Eph. 4:4; 1 Thess. 2:12; 2 Tim. 1:9; see also Heb. 9:15; 1 Pet. 2:9; 2 Pet. 1:10). In his personal worship of God, confession of sin, trust in God's promises, obedience to God's Word, and quest for God's glory, Nehemiah models for us in a most striking way what it means to be "called" by God in this first sense. He is a man impressively alive to God; there is not the least doubt about that.

The second calling is a summons to a task. Paul is speaking of this when he introduces himself to the Roman believers as "Paul . . . called to be an apostle" (Rom. 1:1; cf. 1 Cor. 1:1). Elsewhere he is emphatic that all Christians are gifted for, and thereby called to, some form of service (see Rom. 12:4-6; 1 Cor. 12:7-11; Eph. 4:7-16). This is a line of teaching that has become very familiar, and rightly so, in recent years: all believers are in the Christian ministry, in the sense of being called to find and fulfill the serving role for which God has equipped them. Gifts are given to be used, and a capacity to minister in a particular way constitutes a *prima facie* call to that particular ministry. It was so with Nehemiah, as we shall see.

But how does one find one's own proper ministry task once one has found the Lord? How does God guide us into the specific roles for which he has gifted us? Four factors ordinarily come together in this process.

First, there is the *biblical* factor. This is in a broad sense directional, setting before us goals and guidelines and a scale of values for shaping our lives. The Bible tells us in general terms what is and is not worth doing, what sorts of action God encourages and what sorts he forbids, and what are the things that need to be done in serving the needs of saints and sinners. Hereby it says to us in effect: it is within these limits, in pursuit of these goals, in observance of these priorities, that you will find your ministry. The biblical factor is basic, in the sense that God never leads us to transgress any scriptural boundaries, and if we think we are being so led we need someone with a Bible in his hand to tell us we are deluded.

Then, second, there is the *pneumatic* factor. By this I mean the God-given desires of the spiritually renewed heart, plus any particular nudges that the Holy Spirit may give or any special burdens of concern that he may impose over and above those general desires. We see all these elements in Nehemiah's story: the overall desire for God's glory in Jerusalem that led him to ask how things were in the city (1:2), the burden of specific concern that led him to weep, fast, and pray for its restoration (1:4-11), and "what my God had put in my heart to do for Jerusalem" (2:12)—in other words, the nudging of the Holy Spirit.

Here we reach an area where self-deception is easy and mistakes often get made, but it would be wrong to deprecate openness to the Holy Spirit on that account. Christians vary, in this as in every previous age, as to how much or how little of this nudging they experience (and no sure reason can be given for the variance, save God's good pleasure); but it would be perverse either for those who know more of it to treat as unspiritual those who confessedly know less of it, or for those who know less of it to treat as self-deceived those who claim to know more of it. The classic instance of the Spirit's nudging was on Paul's second missionary journey, when the missionaries were "kept by the Holy Spirit from preaching the word in the province of Asia . . . they tried to enter Bithynia, but the Spirit of Jesus would not allow them to. So they . . . went down to Troas," the port for Greece, the Spirit having thus effectively kept them traveling west on the Troas road (Acts 16:6-8). Then came Paul's vision of the Macedonian calling for help, and God's plan became plain: "we got ready at once to leave for Macedonia, concluding that God had called us [through the nudges and the vision together] to preach the gospel to them" (verse 10). We may not ourselves often be guided by this kind of inner nudge—few of us, I think, are; but to discourage Christians from being open to it, as has sometimes been done, is radically Spirit-quenching.

Third comes the *body* factor: that is, the discipline of submitting such leading towards ministry as we believe ourselves to have received to a cross-section of the Christian fellowship—that is, to the body of Christ in its local manifestation. The reason for this is that our self-judgment as to whether we are fit and able for ministry roles that attract us is not to be trusted; again and again our own self-assessments prove inaccurate. As we shall see, there is a broad hint in our story that Nehemiah was careful to consult others when the idea that he might be the man to rebuild Jerusalem began to take form in his mind.

In the theological college where I taught in England before moving to Canada, it fell to me to interview dozens of men who believed they were called to the pastorate. One thing I was doing in those interviews was trying to assess whether their belief was matched by the temperament, moral character, and gifts that the role requires. I was not the only person attempting this assessment; other faculty members interviewed them as well, and we put our heads together about them after they had gone. In addition, the denomination we served required them to secure testimonials to their ministry potential from their own pastors and to attend a selection conference at which a representative panel of selectors would assess them as we had done. All this was an implementing of the body factor in vocational decision-making. Self-judgments have to be judged and checked by others. When God calls, he equips; when the equipment is lacking, and the potential for role fulfillment is simply not there, God's call is not to what the candidate had in mind, but to something else. And it is within the body that each person's true calling will be discerned.

It can work the other way, too. Persons fitted for the pastorate, or some other ministry, may not realize it and may need to be told that since God has so obviously enriched them with a particular gift or cluster of gifts, they must open themselves to the certainty that he has a ministry for them that matches their gifts and must allow others within the body—pastors, peers, or whoever—to suggest to them what that ministry should be. This, too, is authentic body-life in relation to God's call to serve.

The fourth factor is that of *opportunity*. If the God of providence is calling someone to a particular ministry, he will so overrule that person's situation that he or she will be able to move into that ministry. If circumstances make such a move impossible, the right conclusion is that though God indeed has a ministry for this person, it is not what was originally thought, because of the way the door of circumstances has been closed. As we shall see, the final confirmation that God wanted Nehemiah in Jerusalem, organizing reconstruction, was that in a quite unpredictable way he was given opportunity to go.

A CLEAR CALL

Let us now look directly at the story of Nehemiah's call. Against the background that has just been filled in, I want to pinpoint five significant items that combined to lead Nehemiah from his routine palace job to the hazards of being Jerusalem's governor, builder, morale-raiser, events organizer, and spiritual leader—a killing role he could hardly have sustained had he not been sustained himself by a strong sense that God had sent him to fulfill it and was standing by him as he discharged it.

Consecration to God's service was the first item. This, as England's famous Goons used to say, is where the story really starts. Nehemiah identified himself in prayer as God's "servant" (1:6, 11), and the way of a faithful servant is constantly to ask, as Paul did on the Damascus road, "What shall I do, Lord?" (Acts 22:10). Nehemiah was a man who knew and loved his Lord and was wholly given to his Lord's service. That was his consecration—and also, be it said, his repentance; for the two are one. Repentance is a change of mind issuing in a change of life. Since practical atheism, which disregards God, is natural to fallen human beings, godliness has to be founded on repentance from the start. Repentance means a right-face turn and a quick-march in the direction opposite to that in which we were going before. The original direction was the path of self-service, in the sense of treating yourself as God, the supreme value, and gratifying yourself accordingly. The new direction is a matter of saying good-bye to all that and embracing the service of God instead.

So consecration is repentance renewed and sustained, just as repentance is consecration begun; and here lies the secret of sensitivity to God's call. Paul's familiar summons in Romans 12:1-2 to consecration and transformation leads on to the not-so-familiar point that this is in truth the pathway to discerning God's will, which otherwise you are likely to miss. "I urge you, brothers, in view of God's mercy, to offer your bodies as living sacrifices, holy and pleasing to God. . . . Do not conform any longer to the pattern of this world, but be transformed by the renewing of your mind. *Then you will be able to test and approve what God's will is. . . .*"

The fact we must face is that impenitent and unconsecrated Christians will be out of earshot when God calls them to service, just as they are out of line already, without being fully aware of it, in regard to the imperatives of daily Christian living. Apathy and sluggishness with regard to ordinary obedience brings deafness when God calls to special service. But Nehemiah, a consecrated and repentant servant of God, as his prayer in 1:5-11 shows, was sensitive to God's approach and ready to receive particular guidance. When the bad news floored him and set him praying, he soon found himself suspecting what God's vocational call to him was. Faithful souls become quick on the uptake in these matters. The saga of Nehemiah's achievements starts here.

Communication about people's needs, as just mentioned, was the second item. Bad news came from Jerusalem: walls flattened, gates burned, morale at rock bottom (1:3). Nehemiah had asked anxiously after the state of things in Jerusalem (1:2), because he cared so much about the glory of God and the good of souls there; now he took note that the Jerusalem Jews were in really desperate need. It was, I think, Oswald Chambers who said that the need is not the call but is the occasion for the call, and that is a wise word. There are far more needs in the church and the world than any of us has time or energy to meet, and no one is required to try to relieve them all. Nonetheless, God's call to service will be a call to meet some human need or other, and the sense of what we might and should do to serve God will only crystallize in our hearts out of knowledge of what the needs are. So we should explore the needs that surround us and collect information about them and hold them in our hearts if we want to be led to the particular ministry that God has in mind for us. Cheerful, self-absorbed Christians who fail to do this are not likely to be so led. But Nehemiah's big-hearted burden-bearing for Jerusalem sets us a different example.

Concern for God's cause was the third item. "When I heard these things," Nehemiah tells us, "I sat down and wept. For some days I mourned and fasted and prayed . . ." (1:4). Why? Not only because of the human needs in Jerusalem, but also, and I think primarily, because God was being dishonored as long as Jerusalem lay waste. For Jerusalem was "the holy city" (11:18), the worship center God had chosen "as a dwelling for [his] Name" (1:9)—that is, the appointed place where the reality of his presence would be experienced in love and mercy by those who sought him. Moses had foretold (Dt. 12:4-28) that there would be such a place, and God himself had effectively proclaimed, in his words to Solomon at the dedication of Jerusalem's temple, that this was indeed that place (2 Chr. 7:12-16). The Psalmists understood this; that is why they expressed such excitement at the prospect of going to the temple, and why one of them said, "Better is one day in your courts than a thousand elsewhere" (84:10), and "My soul yearns, even faints for the courts of the LORD; my heart and my flesh cry out for the living God" (verse 2). But none of this could be reality while Jerusalem was in ruins and the temple services were, inevitably, disrupted. Nehemiah identifies with the quest for God's glory and praise, and it is this that prompts his mourning, his fasting (a sign of grieving sympathy, and of seriousness in prayer), and his praying itself. Here we see what I called the biblical and pneumatic factors in divine guidance—namely, Nehemiah's understanding of the revealed will of God regarding Jerusalem, and his deep desire to advance God's honor there, if God would allow him to do that.

Nehemiah's prayer, with its solemn invocation of God in his majesty, its frank admission of the people's sins, its appeal to the covenant promise of restoration for the penitent, and its passionate plea to God as Redeemer to take action, is one of the great prayers of the Bible and could well be studied at great length. At this moment, however, I simply want to call attention to what seems to lie behind it. Verse 11 reads: "O Lord, let your ear be attentive to the prayer of this your servant and to the prayer of your servants who delight in revering your name. Give your servant success today by granting him favor in the presence of this man [the king]." Who are these "servants who delight in revering your name"? They have to be godly friends and associates with whom Nehemiah has shared his concern and who have now joined him in his intense vigil of prayer as he pleads with God to act. And what is the "favor in the presence of this man" that he is praying for? We do not know whether the idea that Nehemiah was the person for the job at Jerusalem had crept into his mind out of his own wish that he might be able to do something to exalt God there, and that he then tested the notion by asking his friends if they thought there was anything in it, or whether his friends first got the idea and pressed it on him as the thing that they should agree to pray for. All we know is that the request for Nehemiah to be sent to Jerusalem became part of the package prayer that they were voicing together, and that Nehemiah was praying it personally, and that he was offering himself for the task of rebuilding the city if God would open the door for him to leave Susa, the Persian capital, for that purpose. Shared concern for God's cause had led the praying group to make this their specific request, and now they were waiting on God to see what he would do. Such was the body factor, as we have called it, in Nehemiah's experience of God's vocational guidance.

Continuance in prayer was the fourth item, and it was then, as it is still, a most important one. For how many days did Nehemiah have to pray, "Give your servant success *today* by granting him favor in the presence of this man"? Nehemiah tells us by the dates he records. In 1:1 we learn that the bad news from Jerusalem came in the month Kislev. In 2:1 we hear that his prayer was answered in the month Nisan. From Kislev (November-December) to Nisan (March-April) is over a hundred days, more than three months, perhaps more than four. For at least three months, then, Nehemiah and his friends waited on God, asking each day that God would act *today*—and nothing happened: nothing, at least, of what they were hoping to see. But something was happening, nonetheless. God was testing their faith, and they were passing the test, it would seem, with flying colors.

We need to realize that what they were asking for was, humanly speaking, so unlikely as to be virtually impossible. For Nehemiah, the royal cupbearer, to be released from his job and dispatched to Jerusalem on a city-building mission would be an unprecedented marvel. Though Nehemiah was evidently a trusted man and one whom the king liked, he was in fact no more than a high-class slave, an alien recruited for palace service, and one whose ministrations were needed there on a daily basis. The cupbearer's responsibility was to taste in advance the wine that the king would drink at the evening banquet, to see whether or not it was poisoned. If it was, the cupbearer would show signs of distress before the banquet began and the king, being thus warned, would abstain and live. (One sees why foreign slaves would be recruited as cupbearers—it was truly high-risk employment.) So the royal cupbearer was a key man, and that was exactly the problem. Slaves had no holidays, and every night of the year Nehemiah was wanted at the palace. There seemed no possibility of his ever being free to go to Jerusalem.

Yet the praying group was sure that theirs was the right request to make, and Nehemiah, himself no doubt the leader of the praying band, explicitly made it his own. Behind this, presumably, was hard-headed awareness on the group's part that Nehemiah was the only person in sight who seemed equal to the task; behind it, too, was certainly a God-given longing in Nehemiah's own heart. So they all prayed steadily in these terms for three months. Wrote Isaiah: "You who call on the LORD, give yourselves no rest, and give him no rest till he establishes Jerusalem and makes her the praise of the earth" (62:6ff.). These believers were doing exactly that.

The story reminds us that even when God's people are praying just the right prayer about the concerns that God himself has laid on their hearts, he still may keep them waiting, because the time he appoints for prayer-answering action is often not as soon as was hoped. So persistence in prayer, proving our seriousness of purpose as we keep our requests before the throne day after day, becomes a vital lesson that all God's people in every age need to learn.

AN AMAZING CALL

The fifth item in the story is circumstantial confirmation. The opening verses of chapter 2 tell how Nehemiah's prayer for "favor in the sight of this man" was finally answered, and how the former royal cupbearer found himself traveling west as the new governor of the province of Trans-Euphrates (so NIV; "the province Beyond the River," as most translations render it; "West-of-Euphrates Province," as GNV vividly says) with an official mandate to rebuild Jerusalem. This was all that Nehemiah had hoped, and more. The story is a startling one, and we should look at it carefully.

At the outset we face a problem of interpretation, over which the commentators divide. The king, Nehemiah tells us, noticed a look of distress on his cupbearer's face, was struck by it (for "I had not been sad in his presence before"), and diagnosed it, correctly, as sorrow of heart (2:1-2), which was a direct invitation to Nehemiah to tell him what the trouble was. Had Nehemiah planned this—taking the gamble of deliberately putting on a sad face so that the king would notice and make the inquiry—waiting (this has been suggested) for the day when the queen would be dining with the king (2:6) so that the king would be in a mood of maximum mellowness for the conversation Nehemiah hoped to start? Or was the sad expression unconscious and involuntary, so that Nehemiah was not expecting the king to address him as he did and so had to reply in a relatively unpremeditated way? The bare statement "I had not been sad in his presence before" does not decide this question; nor does the further statement, "I was very much afraid" following the royal inquiry (2:2); nor does Nehemiah's "arrow prayer" ("I prayed to the God of heaven") prior to answering the king's "What is it you want?" (2:4). Since palace etiquette required all servants to look happy in the king's presence (a compliment to the boss, you could call it, as if the royal presence would always produce total joy), and since failure here was thought treasonable, an insult to the crown, and could be punished with death if the king so decided, we can see why Nehemiah would have been afraid, even if he had himself engineered the exchange in the way suggested. And the wisdom of praying before speaking, when what he was to say was bound to have a major effect one way or another, would have been obvious to him in either case. So the fact that he prayed ("Lord, this is important; help me here and now to say my piece right") need not mean that the question had taken him by surprise, though it could mean that. The problem remains unresolved.

John White argues that Nehemiah "would not request God's 'favor in the presence of' King Artaxerxes unless he planned something risky"—namely, the sad face.[2] But surely the point of Nehemiah's request was that only Artaxerxes could give him permission to exchange cupbearing for construction, and it is gratuitous to read any more into it than this. And the suggestion that Nehemiah, almost certainly a full-bearded man, could put on a sad face to order seems doubtful. Pulling down the corners of your mouth to make yourself look glum often goes unnoticed if you wear a beard. The king's opening remark was, "Why does your face look so sad when you are not ill?" Trouble of heart shows itself in eyes full of pain, drawn and lined features, sunken cheeks, and a haggard look; none of these things can be easily produced at will, though all of them will appear, spontaneously and unawares, on the faces of persons in distress.

It seems to me, therefore, much more natural to suppose that what Nehemiah's narrative is telling us is this: that his three-month prayer for favor in the king's presence was accompanied by complete uncertainty as to how the question of his going to Jerusalem could ever be raised; that he had no idea what volumes his face, which as a good courtier he was trying to keep happy, was actually speaking about the state of his heart; that he was not expecting to hear the king diagnose sadness of heart and quiz him as to what the trouble was, and he was certainly not manipulating the situation by putting on a sad look in order to be noticed and questioned; and that in retrospect the entire episode appeared to him as a fantastic answer to prayer: he had asked for the seemingly impossible, and it had happened. He had not himself dared mention the thing that was on his heart, but the king had brought it up and had been as forthcoming as anyone could imagine, promoting Nehemiah from cupbearing for as long as he wished, giving him a safe-conduct and requisition orders for the raw materials he would need, and actually appointing him provincial governor, thus giving him unassailable official standing (this is explicit in 5:14, and implicit in Nehemiah's request for timber "for the residence I will occupy"—i.e., a governor's house, 2:8). Circumstantial confirmation of his call to serve was thus as complete as it could possibly be; the opportunity factor was now fully in line with the biblical, pneumatic, and body factors, as these applied in Nehemiah's case. Well might Nehemiah now celebrate "the gracious hand of my God . . . upon me" (2:8, 18). Now he knew, beyond any shadow of doubt, that God was sending him to Jerusalem, and that God would be with him in the hazards, the uncertainties, and the expected rough ride in which the task of reconstruction would involve him.

This development was truly amazing, for it involved a direct reversal of Artaxerxes' own previous policy. Ezra 4:7-23 tells how some years before he had been petitioned by leaders of city-states in the Jerusalem area to stop the building of Jerusalem's walls and had done as asked. But "the king's heart is in the hand of the LORD; he directs it like a watercourse wherever he pleases" (Prov. 21:1). On the spur of the moment Artaxerxes decided to make Nehemiah governor of Trans-Euphrates and give him authority to rebuild, and so Nehemiah's course was set for the next several years. Prayer changes things!

A CONSTRAINING CALL

The constraint of God's call to any form of ministry is great. Of his apostolic vocation Paul wrote: "when I preach the gospel, I cannot boast, for I am compelled to preach. Woe to me if I do not preach the gospel!" (1 Cor. 9:16). Nehemiah felt himself equally under compulsion, now that God's call to him was clear, and tackled the task of restoring Jerusalem with single-minded, whole-hearted enthusiasm. As we shall see, he focused his goals, planned thoroughly for their accomplishment, worked hard for long hours, dealt patiently and wisely with each problem as it arose, resisted distractions, and refused to be discouraged at any stage. He took his calling seriously and fulfilled it gloriously, and in this he is a model to all who serve in God's church. We shall do well to face the questions that his example prompts.

Do we in fact start where he started, with the same passion for God's glory and the same burden of concern and distress when we contemplate the broken-down state of God's church?

> How few the strong men in these days who can weep at the evils and abominations of the times! How rare those who, seeing the desolations of Zion, are sufficiently interested and concerned for the welfare of the church to mourn! Mourning and weeping over the decay of religion, the decline of revival power, and the fearful inroads of worldliness in the church are almost an unknown quantity. . . . Nehemiah was a mourner in Zion.[3]

These words of E. M. Bounds, written almost a century ago, apply more directly today than they did in Bounds's own time. Are we willing to learn to pray for the struggling communities of God's people as Nehemiah prayed for the Jews, and to accept with Nehemiah any change of circumstances and any risk that may be involved in rendering the needed service?

Are we proceeding as he proceeded, putting God first, others second, and ourselves last as we seek to fulfil our call to ministry? Do we act in a disinterested way, not seeking ease or personal advantage but simply making it our business to love and serve our Lord by loving and serving our neighbor, leaving it to the Lord to look after us as we concentrate on the tasks he has given us?

And when God is pleased to use us as a means of good to his people, shall we with Nehemiah give him the glory and the praise for what has happened and decline to take the credit for ourselves? Shall we humbly acknowledge the gracious hand of our God upon us, and the gracious kindness of our God in using us, rather than conceitedly supposing that the result is due to our own skills and talents and wisdom and gifts and experience?

Before going any further, let us examine ourselves. We need to.

CHAPTER THREE

Man-Management I: Getting Going

Here is the next segment of Nehemiah's story. Once clear on his call, he got down to business. He was not a man who let the grass grow under his feet.

So I went to the governors of Trans-Euphrates and gave them the king's letters. The king had also sent army officers and cavalry with me.

When Sanballat the Horonite and Tobiah the Ammonite official heard about this, they were very much disturbed that someone had come to promote the welfare of the Israelites.

I went to Jerusalem, and after staying there three days I set out during the night with a few men. I had not told anyone what my God had put in my heart to do for Jerusalem. There were no mounts with me except the one I was riding on.

By night I went out through the Valley Gate toward the Jackal Well and the Dung Gate, examining the walls of Jerusalem, which had been broken down, and its gates, which had been destroyed by fire. Then I moved on toward the Fountain Gate and the King's Pool, but there was not enough room for my mount to get through; so I went up the valley by night, examining the wall. Finally, I turned back and reentered through the Valley Gate. The officials did not know where I had gone or what I was doing, because as yet I had said nothing to the Jews or the priests or nobles or officials or any others who would be doing the work.

Then I said to them, "You see the trouble we are in: Jerusalem lies in ruins, and its gates have been burned with fire. Come, let us rebuild the wall of Jerusalem, and we will no longer be in disgrace." I also told them about the gracious hand of my God upon me and what the king had said to me.

They replied, "Let us start rebuilding." So they began this good work.

But when Sanballat the Horonite, Tobiah the Ammonite official and Geshem the Arab heard about it, they mocked and ridiculed us. "What is this you are doing?" they asked. "Are you rebelling against the king?"

I answered them by saying, "The God of heaven will give us success. We his servants will start rebuilding, but as for you, you have no share in Jerusalem or any claim or historic right to it."

(Nehemiah 2:9-20)

The task, as we have seen, was to rebuild the walls of Jerusalem, so that the life of the city could be reestablished. Until the walls were up, nothing else could be done. With its walls down, Jerusalem had no defense against raiders and invaders and was no place to make a home. Hence many of the citizens had moved out (7:4), and now temple worship could not be maintained and morale had sunk to rock bottom.

In this, let us note, Jerusalem is a picture of Christian churches generally in the modern West. Weakness, disillusionment, and the melting away of adherents is the story everywhere. In Asia and Africa and Latin America the gospel advances and the church grows, but in the Protestant world of Britain, Europe, North America, and Australia the secularizing of community life and the faltering of theologians, church leaders, and ordinary clergy has left the majority of congregations in a very low state. Abandonment of the historic belief in a holy Creator who graciously saves sinners through atonement and new birth is common still, as it has been for the past century, and whenever fidelity to the biblical faith ceases, spiritual vitality quickly drains away. Overall the Western church has shriveled and shrunk; it has ceased to count as a community force; the faith of which God made it trustee is largely unknown to the man in the street, and when known it is largely ignored; and the godliness that the church once set forth as true humanness is rated in popular culture as a comic, old-fashioned oddity. The church appears as a ruined city, like Sarajevo or Beirut after the fighting, and like Jerusalem as Nehemiah found it, and a tremendous rebuilding job awaits anyone who still cares about its welfare. In such rebuilding, the reconstruction of biblical belief will be the first and basic task.

Nehemiah's vocation was to take the lead in the literal rebuilding of Jerusalem, and his book now moves on from the story of his call to tell us how he did it. As an adventure story, it is an exciting read, for Nehemiah is a top-class narrator; but over and above that, the book is Holy Scripture, and Holy Scripture is inspired, and inspiration means God-givenness, and God-givenness means that we should hear and read the book as the word of God himself teaching, preaching, telling the story, witnessing to himself in and through the words of Nehemiah's witness to him. God is the primary author of all Scripture, historical narratives no less than prophetic sermons or apostolic letters or Ecclesiastes' broodings before the throne or David's poems of praise and petition addressed to the throne's occupant directly. The books of Nehemiah and Ezra, the latter reading, as we have observed, like an introduction to the former, cover the period from the exiles' return to the reestablishing of Jerusalem as a going concern, and we shall find in Nehemiah's narrative specifically much that bears on the task of building up God's church today. The God who ruled over Nehemiah's journal-keeping and memoir-writing planned it so, and in learning from Nehemiah we are learning from our Maker in person.

In his role as pioneer in the reconstructing of Jerusalem, Nehemiah illustrates many of the realities of spiritual leadership in the Christian church. We see in him the zeal for God and the love for people, plus the readiness to challenge his challengers and to oppose personal opposition, that every leader needs. We see in him also the true essence of leadership, as an enabling of others to achieve; the real loneliness of leadership, as the leader holds fast the vision of the goal of which his followers are losing sight; and the burning zeal for God that the leader must ever show forth as a model for those he leads. All the great leaders of God's people in the Bible story (think, for instance, of Moses, David, and Paul) displayed these qualities to some degree, and Jesus himself, as leader both of the twelve and of a larger group of real though less intimate disciples, displayed them all to a very high degree. And then, in Nehemiah as in these others, a further requirement of leadership can be seen—namely, a willingness to work extremely hard under pressure, with a concurrent concern to move others to do the same. Let us explore this a little further.

WORK

The noun "work" recurs again and again, like a drumbeat, in Nehemiah's story of the building of the wall. "As yet I had said nothing to the Jews . . . who would be doing the *work*" (2:16). "They began this good *work*" (2:18). "Their nobles would not put their shoulders to the *work*" (3:5; a different word in the Hebrew). "Our enemies said . . . 'we will . . . put an end to the *work*'" (4:11). "We all returned . . . each to his own *work*" (4:15). "Half of my men did the *work*. . . . Those who carried materials did their *work* with one hand" (4:16-17). "Then I said . . . 'The *work* is extensive'" (4:19). "So we continued the *work*" (4:21). "I devoted myself to the *work* on this wall. All my men were assembled there for the *work*" (5:16). "'I am carrying on a great project [*work* in the Hebrew]. . . . Why should the *work* stop . . . ?'" (6:3). "They were . . . thinking, 'Their hands will get too weak for the *work*'" (6:9). "Our enemies . . . realized that this *work* had been done with the help of our God" (6:16).

These are all, of course, references to the specific labor of erecting Jerusalem's walls, and we could, if we wished, leave the matter there. But it is instructive to probe a bit deeper. What is "work" as such? And how does the Bible regard it? What general truths about work lie behind these particular texts? And what can we learn from this narrative about work as part of our own lives?

First, let us be clear that when the Bible talks about work it has in view much more than what we do for money or gain, what we call our job or our employment. In the Bible, work as such means any exertion of effort that aims at producing a new state of affairs. Such exertions involve our creativity, which is part of God's image in us, and which needs to be harnessed and expressed in action if our nature is to be properly fulfilled. So, for instance, homemaking, sweeping snow, obeying orders, practicing for a performance, darning socks, and answering letters are all focused, intentional exertions that count as work, though none of them necessarily involves contractual employment. Conversely, warbling under the shower to express your sense of euphoria at the feel of the hot water is not work, no matter how much energy you put into it and how much noise you make. If, however, your warbling was learning a part to sing in a choir, that would be work, because of its purpose. Work in the biblical sense is always goal-oriented; it is action with an end in view.

Second, let us be clear that the Bible envisages life as a rhythm of work and rest (generally, labor by day and sleep by night; labor for six days and rest on the seventh) and does not distinguish between spiritual and secular work as if these belonged in two separate compartments. The Bible teaches, rather, that we should plan and live our life as a unity in which nothing is secular and everything is in a real sense sacred, because everything is being done for the glory of God—that is, to show appreciation for what he has made, to please him by loving obedience to his commands, and to advance his honor and praise among his creatures, starting with the homage and adoration that we render to him ourselves. "Whether you eat or drink or whatever you do, do it all for the glory of God" (1 Cor. 10:31). Nothing is to be viewed as less than sacred; there is to be no compartmentalizing of our daily doings; work is to be a unifying reality that holds all our life together.

The third thing we must be clear on is that God made us all for work. Human nature only finds fulfillment and contentment when in this broad sense of the word we have work to do. This appears from the creation story, which tells us that God put Adam "in the Garden of Eden to work it and take care of it" (Gen. 2:15). The work would have given him great pleasure and no pain; thorns and thistles disrupting cultivation, and sweat and tears because of barren fields and failed harvests, only came in through the curse that followed the Fall (3:17-19). The work would have required constant thought and effort, as every gardener knows very well; yet it would have been happy partnership with God all the way, ordering the natural life and shaping the spontaneous growth that God gives to trees and plants, and Adam would have perceived himself as fulfilling his human calling to be, in J. R. R. Tolkien's word, a "sub-creator" under God. Gardeners still have moments of great satisfaction at what grows under their hand, and everyone's work everywhere would have felt fulfilling in this way all the time had there been no fall.

God, it seems, has ordained work to be our destiny, both here and hereafter. (Hereafter? Yes; in the heavenly city "his servants will serve him" and "reign for ever and ever" [Rev. 22:3, 5], all of which means active work.) What was his reason for planning our lives this way? I think we see the answer when we note what happens as we work. We then discover our potential as craftsmen, learning to do things and developing skills, which is fascinating. We also discover the potential of God's world as raw material for us to use, manage, and bring into shape, which is fascinating too. God's command to Adam and Eve to fill and subdue the earth (Gen. 1:28) is sometimes called "the cultural mandate," because every attempt to fulfill it at once produces culture— that is, a pattern of community life based, as all cultures are, on work with a purpose. Work as a way of life that we approve, embrace, and pursue for the glory of God generates within us a spirit of praise to him, both for the wonders of creation outside us and for the creativity that our work draws out of us. Furthermore, work brings joy in the experience of making and managing; work fosters wisdom and maturity in the way we run things, including our relationships with other people (in which also we are meant to be creative); work leads to an increase of affection and goodwill towards others as we harness our skills to serve them; and work develops ingenuity and resourcefulness in finding ways to tap into the powers and processes that surround us.

Had God not required us, made as we are, to work in his

world, the experience of fulfillment that these things engender would not be ours; and if, made as we are, we should become work-shy and give ourselves to pursuing leisure and amusement instead, we should sentence ourselves to deep-level dissatisfaction with life. No form of work can guarantee that virtue, love, and joy will become ours, but we need not expect that virtue, love, and joy will ever mark us out if our lives have in them no form of work. Nehemiah, Moses, David, Paul, and Jesus beckon us down a different path, a path of purposeful effort, as indeed does the entire New Testament, with its insistence that Christians must constantly practice "good works" (Mt. 5:16; 2 Cor. 9:8; Eph. 2:10; 1 Tim. 6:18; 2 Tim. 3:17; Tit. 2:7, 14; 3:1, 8, 14; Heb. 10:24; etc.).

We are here thinking of work, as we have said, in a much wider and more basic sense than paid employment, but it would be wrong not to notice as we proceed that one great social evil in the modern West is the ongoing lack of paid employment for something like 10 percent of the work force—in other words, the actual unemployment of many millions at any one time. Inability to find paid work is demoralizing and depressing, as well as financially and spiritually impoverishing. The unemployed need all the sympathy and help that Christians can give, both to retain their self-respect and also to go on using their natural creativity in informal ways, which their inner frustration tempts them not to do.

In Nehemiah 2:18 the rebuilding of Jerusalem's wall is classified as "this good work." What makes "work"—a specific piece of work, or a particular activity—"good"—good, that is, in God's estimation? The answer is, two things coinciding: first, its intrinsic character; second, the agent's motivation. The action itself must be biblically right; that is, it must be something that God has shown he wants done. Also, the motive of the person performing it must be right—namely, love to God and man, and a purpose of advancing God's glory. Nehemiah's tackling of the task of reconstruction is a textbook example: the job cried out to be done, and Nehemiah's goal was to glorify God and serve the people by doing it.

In everything we tackle, we should be consciously doing our best, for only so can we glorify God. John White has some telling words on this.

> . . . maybe you are just bored. Your boredom may arise from unbelief or something akin to unbelief—lack of vision. You do not have a clearly defined goal ahead of you. You are drifting. Pray about your work. Ask the Holy Spirit to give you a definite goal for the next three months. Then drive for that goal.
>
> Or perhaps you do not like the work you are called to do. You feel unfit for it. You could slave at something else, but your own work is too unattractive. Remember the verse, "Whatever your hand finds to do, do it with all your might" (Eccles. 9:10). You will be surprised how enjoyable a task becomes when you master it. Make it your aim to do your daily job superbly, and you will turn drudgery into a craft and a craft into an art. Nothing is so boring as sloppy work.[1]

Nehemiah, as we shall see, models this focused, intentional, high-aiming approach to work in a very striking way.

The work that glorifies God, then, is hard work. But is it not easy—dreadfully easy—to work too hard and become a workaholic or induce burnout or a coronary thrombosis or some other chilling consequence of doing too much? Once more I quote physician and psychiatrist John White, who under the heading "The Bogeyman of Overwork" writes as follows:

> Work does not produce nervous breakdowns, despite what anyone may have told you to the contrary. Work

as hard as you like and as long as you like. If you're in normal health, you come to little harm. . . .

Why? Because it is tension that kills, not work. It is getting caught in the Christian rat race that does the damage. It is the desperate fight to keep up a front with Christian friends or with the Christian public, to appear smilingly spiritual and "produce" spiritually when you know all the while that your true inner life does not measure up to your exterior image.

Pastor White then speaks directly about workaholism:

Sometimes we work too much not because the work is essential, but because we are driven by fear—rather than sustained by faith. Workaholics are driven. Work for them is not an expression of faith but a search for peace . . . workaholics try to keep their consciences clean by working. Consequently they work too much and become slaves to their own neuroticism. Workaholics cannot easily rest; they begin to look haunted when relaxing. . . .

The Scriptures do not encourage this sort of driven-ness. "In vain you rise early and stay up late, toiling for food to eat—for he grants sleep to those he loves" (Ps. 127:2). Nehemiah . . . was deeply aware that labor is futile if it is not in and with the Lord. Nehemiah worked hard when hard work was needed *because he knew God's hand was on him* (2:8, 18), not because he suffered a neu-rotic need to achieve.[2]

WORK AND PRAYER

Nehemiah was a hard worker who, as we shall see, moti-vated others by his words and inspired them by his exam-ple to work hard with him. He was also, as we have already noticed, very much a man of prayer. He tells us his story in a way that highlights both his skill as a mobilizer and his passion as a petitioner, and he does so with the same breath-taking, God-focused matter-of-factness that marks Augustine's *Confessions* and Bunyan's *Grace Abounding* and Whitefield's and Wesley's *Journals* and the autobiographies of George Muller and C. H. Spurgeon. Like them, Nehemiah is able to write about himself in a way that does not call attention to himself, because he fixes the reader's attention throughout where his own is fixed already—namely, on God, the God who in answer to prayer does wonders, the God whom the writer adores. It is natural, however, that as we read Nehemiah's story we should ask ourselves how praying to God and working for God relate. Part of the answer, I urge, is that our praying determines the quality of our working, just as our working reflects the quality of our praying. Nehemiah's narrative seems to illustrate this very clearly.

William Temple said somewhere that whereas we think our real work is our activity, to which prayer is an adjunct, our praying is our real work, and our activity is the index of how we have done it. Surely Temple is right. For real prayer—prayer, that is, that centers on the hallowing of God's name and the doing of his will—has, among its other effects, a reflex effect. It purifies the heart; it purges our attitudes and motives; it melts down all the self-centeredness, self-sufficiency, and self-reliance that as fallen creatures we bring to it, and programs us to work humbly, in a God-honoring, God-fearing, God-dependent way. We need to remember that in God's sight motivation is an integral element in action: the Lord looks not only on the outward behavior but also on the heart, and any motivation that exalts self will render our work rotten at the core from his point of view. (Remember the Pharisees, and Jesus' words about them!) Because of the self-absorbed habits of our sinful hearts, the only way to anything like pure motives is to pray persistently about the things we do and ask ourselves constantly before the Lord why we are doing them and how they fit in with God's glory and the good of his people. This is the path to purer hearts than we could hope to have otherwise. I see Nehemiah as an example of this, for it looks as if he followed the above procedure all the time.

Nehemiah's rule of action seems to have been: first pray, then act, then pray again. Note once more the way that prayer punctuates his narrative of the building of the wall. Prayer for the welfare of Jerusalem was the seed-bed out of which the whole enterprise grew (1:5-11). Prayer for help when the king required him to say what his trouble was led to his being sent to Jerusalem (2:4-6). Prayer was his recourse again when Sanballat and Tobiah ridiculed the first stages of the rebuilding ("hear us, O our God, for we are despised . . . they have thrown insults in the face of the builders," 4:4-5). When he and his colleagues learned of the plot to attack the city and flatten the wall once more, "we prayed to our God" (4:9) before taking defense measures. First things first! Prayer before making a move is surely the right order. Then in 6:9 we read: "They were all trying to frighten us . . . but I prayed, 'Now strengthen my hands.'" Having thus prayed, and having seen prayer answered at each stage, Nehemiah was well entitled to say of the completed wall, "This work had been done with the help of our God" (6:16). So indeed it was.

And what was the reflex effect of Nehemiah's prayers, which, as he wants us to see, God so signally answered? It looks as if, by centering his heart on God's glory, by quenching his fears and raising him above panicky confusions, by distancing him from his anger, by enabling him to maintain the cool practicality that was his special gift, and by keeping him poised and eager in the service of his divine King, Nehemiah's praying qualified and equipped him for leadership in a very direct way. To be sure, this reflex effect of prayer on character and personal potential is not an automatic process but is wrought in sovereignty by the Holy Spirit; nonetheless, we are only likely ever to see such enhancings of natural powers when people pray. Prayer is the ordinary means whereby the gift of wisdom in all its aspects (which is what we are really discussing here) is given. As James says: "If any of you lacks wisdom, he should ask God . . . and it will be given to him" (1:5).

Abraham Lincoln said on one occasion: "I have been driven many times to my knees by the overwhelming conviction that I had nowhere else to go. My own wisdom and that of those about me seemed insufficient. . . ."[3] Long before Lincoln, this was the path Nehemiah trod, and the secret of the quality of his leadership in reestablishing Jerusalem lay here. Well does James Boice observe: "Charles Swindoll has it right, I think, when he refers to Nehemiah as 'A Leader— From the Knees Up!'"[4]

LEADERSHIP AND PARTNERSHIP

The particular work to which God had called Nehemiah was to get Jerusalem's ruined walls rebuilt. This was a huge job. The circuit of the walls was more than a mile, and the new wall needed to be three or four feet thick, more perhaps at ground level, and fifteen to twenty feet high. Rebuilding would be a massive operation, only possible if tackled as a grand-scale cooperative enterprise. Nehemiah made it happen; within days of his coming to Jerusalem, apparently, he had set everything in motion, and the wall was completed in just over seven weeks. It was a staggering achievement.

How, we ask, did Nehemiah do it? There is no secret here; Nehemiah's memoirs tell the whole story, and what they reveal is that, over and above faith and prayer, God-given leader-like wisdom marked his action at every stage. Specifically, he applied two principles that all pastoral leaders today and tomorrow must learn to apply if the churches or Christian groups committed to their care are to be truly built up. The first principle was that of partnership, whereby Nehemiah first motivated the Jerusalemites to snap out of their apathy and hopelessness and commit themselves to work with him wholeheartedly on the project, and then created a setup in which all the workers were able to feel personally important to the project as it went along.

The second principle was that of planning, whereby through harrowing ups and downs Nehemiah was able to sustain their confidence in ultimate success by being seen to have everything under control. Mobilizing, organizing, supervising, and encouraging, Nehemiah galvanized the deadbeats of Jerusalem into well-planned exertions that at once began to transform the entire scene and that did not cease till the whole task was accomplished.

These two principles together epitomize the worldly wisdom of all history's great leaders, men like Alexander the Great, Oliver Cromwell, Napoleon Bonaparte, and Winston Churchill, and they epitomize equally the spiritual wisdom of men like Nehemiah, who humanly belongs in the same class as these four, but whose special role was to find followers whom he would lead out of spiritual coma towards greatness in the kingdom of God.

Coma—I think we may say with confidence that this is a fitting word for the total lack of vision and vitality, and the total inertia so far as God's service was concerned, that Nehemiah faced when he reached Jerusalem. The plight of today's refugees, humans with no security and no future, victims of other people's power struggles, with everything in their lives now combining to assure them they are worthless, is the nearest parallel we can draw. The spirit of those who hung on, improvising an existence for themselves amid Jerusalem's ruins, was thoroughly broken, and hope was dead; the dull routine of trying to arrange for the next meal was all that was left to them. It is no wonder, then, that for the first few days Nehemiah told no one "what my God had put in my heart to do" for the city (2:12; cf. v. 16); the knee-jerk reaction would have been derisive laughter at the newcomer's naiveté, and having made fun of Nehemiah's ideas at first hearing the Jerusalemites would have found it much harder at a later stage to take them seriously.

Many leaders, or would-be leaders, have jeopardized their best schemes by publishing them prematurely, so that they received ridicule and rejection from the people who were to be benefited by them, but who were not yet able to appreciate them. (How often does this happen when zealous new pastors move into moribund congregations! And how ruinous to the new ministry such a mistake can be!) "Do not throw your pearls to pigs," said Jesus: "if you do, they may trample them under their feet, and then turn and tear you to pieces" (Mt. 7:6). But Nehemiah did not make that mistake. In 2:11-20 we see how in fact he got the people going; there he allows us to follow him through the series of stages that clearly constituted his game plan from the start.

Step 1 in Nehemiah's plan was *definition*, as it always must be in any successful strategy for accomplishing anything whatever. The first need is to get clear in one's mind what exactly the task is, what are its size and scope, what are its parameters and limits. Then your goals—long-term, mid-term, and short-term—will be clearly set and you will know just what you are aiming at: what you are doing, where you are going, and what will be involved in getting there. Only when a job has been thus defined can you realistically work out means to your end, and only when you are clear about both the end and the means can you expect anyone else to have confidence in your project. Nehemiah's first step, therefore, was to make a tour of inspection, so that he could define the task realistically and in detail, on a basis of direct knowledge.

Accordingly, having spent three days settling down as governor, which meant, of course, chief administrator of Jerusalem's affairs, he rode out by night on a mule or donkey, accompanied by a few men on foot as a guard, "examining the walls of Jerusalem, which had been broken down, and its gates, which had been destroyed by fire" (2:13). He gives us the details of his route: it appears that he only got round half the length of the walls or less,[5] but that was enough for his purpose. He stresses that the trip was secret: "the officials did not know where I had gone or what I was doing" (2:16). He was in fact doing necessary homework, observing firsthand how the land lay and how much damage there was to be repaired. More likely than not, he had never been in Jerusalem before and really was starting from scratch; and he was wise enough not to leave it to others to act as his eyes, but to go and look at everything for himself. He knew that he would not be able to motivate the people for rebuilding unless he could show himself fully abreast of the way things were; so he took appropriate action to clue himself in.

Definition of the task based on observation of the wrecked walls, and preparing a detailed strategy for re-erecting them, were necessary steps before Nehemiah could hope to carry the locals with him when he went public with his proposals. Faith and planning must go together. When zealous Christians with strong faith allow themselves to go goofy when it comes to orchestrating a cherished enterprise, failure regularly results—not because God is not responsive to faith, but because it is not his way to applaud and bless goofiness. The realism of Nehemiah's careful preparation is the true model for us to follow when we are called to make things happen for God.

Step 2 in Nehemiah's plan was *motivation*, animation for action as we might express it, and here Nehemiah showed himself very shrewd. We watched him gather the information he needed before announcing his intentions; now we see him with everything in hand, having calculated the cost and having equipped himself to answer questions about how the work would be done, springing on the Jerusalemites— Jews, priests, nobles, officials, the "them" of verse 17—his audacious proposal and asking them to join him in implementing it. "Then I said to them, 'You see the trouble we are in: Jerusalem lies in ruins, and its gates have been burned with fire. Come, let us rebuild the wall of Jerusalem, and we will no longer be in disgrace.'"

Note how thoroughly Nehemiah, the new governor just arrived from the Persian capital, identified with his fellow-Jews whom he had been sent to govern. "He does not play the visiting official from Susa, saying, 'You people are in a mess, and I have come to help you'. Rather it is, 'You see the bad situation *we* are in.' He is one of them."[6]

Note too how purposefully, having thus declared his solidarity with them, he stirred them up to action. "'Come, let *us* rebuild . . . and *we* will no longer be in disgrace.'"

All real leaders are masters of motivation. Think, for example, of Winston Churchill making his first speech as Prime Minister in World War II, when France was falling, Britain's power was at its lowest ebb, and capitulating seemed the only sensible option. "I have nothing to offer but blood, toil, tears and sweat. . . . What is our aim? I can answer in one word: Victory—victory at all costs, victory in spite of all terror, victory however long and hard the road may be. . . ." And later, when invasion seemed certain: "We shall defend our island, whatever the cost may be; we shall fight on the beaches, we shall fight on the landing-grounds, we shall fight in the fields and in the streets, we shall fight in the hills; we shall never surrender. . . ."[7] No speeches ever generated a national will to go on fighting more effectively than did Churchill's wartime speeches, and one major factor in that national will was confidence that with a leader of this caliber Britain could hope to win, as by the mercy of God, in company with the Commonwealth nations, the United States of America, and Russia, Britain finally did.

Nehemiah, too, was a master of motivating communication, and he too, like Churchill, made a decisive impact with his first speech as leader of his people. Nehemiah projected the prospect of ending Jerusalem's disgrace and then, at what we would call the psychological moment, revealed how God had led him to his present eminence and how, by a complete reversal of earlier imperial policy, the Persian monarch had actually given the green light for the rebuilding of the walls. "I also told them about the gracious hand of my God upon me and what the king had said to me." Nehemiah's testimony had an immediate effect; his confidence was infectious, the crowd caught the vision, and hope suddenly soared. "They replied, 'Let us start rebuilding.' So they began this good work" (2:18). The great restoration was off and running. Motivated and animated by what they had heard, "the people worked with all their heart" (4:6).

Step 3 in Nehemiah's plan was *organization*, a skill of which he was evidently a master. The roster of builders in chapter 3 shows the work delegated to some forty-one separate groups. By this division of labor all parts of the wall were being rebuilt together. All kinds of people pitched in: priests (including the high priest, 3:1), Levites, temple servants, goldsmiths, merchants, officials, private individuals, women (3:12), and men from Jericho, Tekoa, Gibeon, Mizpah, and other towns in Jerusalem's hinterland. "Not only did Nehemiah coordinate the work so that no gaps were left and all worked closely to one another," writes James Boice, "but he also seems to have arranged the work in part for the convenience and motivation of the workers." (Man-management at its best!) "Many were assigned to (or chose) portions of the wall in front of or directly adjacent to their houses— the priests rebuilding the area near the temple (vv. 1, 28), the temple servants the area near their dwelling on the temple mount (v. 26), Jedaiah the portion of the wall 'opposite his house' (v. 10), Benjamin and Hassub the portion of the wall 'in front of their house' (v. 23), and so on. This would be convenient for all, since no time would be lost in commuting back and forth or in going home for lunch. And it would ensure good work. A person would be certain to build strong walls where his own house needed to be protected."[8] Brilliant! Nehemiah organized with masterly skill.

Chapter 3 does not name Nehemiah as builder of any one part of the wall, but in a deep and obvious sense he must be honored as builder of the whole of it. For having shared out the work among those he had motivated and mobilized to do it, he now gave himself to the task of supervising, coordinating, acting as site manager, and protecting both the building and the builders—setting a round-the-clock watch when invasion threatened (4:7-9), stationing clan units of able-bodied warriors at key points to repel invaders (4:13-15), keeping detachments of armed men constantly at the ready (4:16, 21), and having everyone, including himself, sleep on-the-ready in the city itself, so as to be a guard force by night as well as a work force by day, poised to rally at once to Nehemiah's trumpeter (4:18, 20) should he sound an emergency. The fact that the governor, who might have left Jerusalem each night for the equivalent of a five-star hotel in a quiet outlying village, chose to stay and tough it out with the troops and the work gangs must have gone far to sustain morale during some very exhausting weeks. It is, of course, tremendously heartening when a leader is seen to be sharing the hardships of those he leads. Nehemiah understood the responsibilities of the leader's role and did not fail at this point.

John White waxes lyrical in contemplating this:

> Nehemiah is not the type of leader who avoids sweating. . . . Nehemiah refused to spare himself. . . .

> Nehemiah slaved with abandon. . . . Nothing has ever
> been done for God without work. . . . Paul "worked
> harder than all of them" (1 Cor. 15:10). . . . Wesley often
> preached several times a day. . . . Jesus . . . once sank into
> such exhausted slumber on a boat that even a Galilean
> storm failed to rouse him . . . the one thing all great
> women and men have in common is that they worked.[9]

This point is one we should not hesitate to take.

Getting going is regularly the hardest part of any enterprise. In the days when horses hauled four-wheeled wagons and cars to and fro in the shunting yards of England's railways, it was reckoned that a good horse could pull up to six empties once they were on the move, but could only start one from rest. In our day, when the attempt is made to reanimate a shrinking, inert local church, where nothing of significance has changed for years, getting going still proves to be the hardest part. Nehemiah's pattern of definition, motivation, and organization, choosing the right moment to say and do things and accepting visible involvement in the slog and strain of generating purposeful movement and turning that movement into a communal habit, holds the secret, if we have the wit to latch on to it. Nehemiah's own success here was not quite total. He tells us that the nobles of Tekoa, out of pride apparently, and perhaps apathy too, would not join in the enterprise, though ordinary Tekoans and men from Jericho, which was further from Jerusalem than Tekoa, were doing so (3:2, 5). But it was spectacular success nonetheless, and much of that under God was undoubtedly due to the skill in man-management that Nehemiah showed from the start.

THE NEED TO ORGANIZE

A further word about organization is appropriate at this point. Organizing is a skill for which some have a natural bent, but which all can learn by taking a little trouble.

Oddly, however, those who theorize and strategize about the renewing and reviving of churches are divided about it. Some who think the church will be renewed by preaching, and others who look for its renewal to Christians' Spirit-baptism and an outpouring of gifts, particularly tongues, prophecy, power to heal, and capacities for supernatural discernment, decry organization as a focus of carnal confidence and an intrinsically Spirit-quenching development. At the opposite extreme, books are written and journals published that treat organization as the elixir of life and set forth organizational patterns for pastors and their flocks in a way that implies guaranteed growth, both in quantity and in quality, if the instructions are followed. What is the truth here? It seems to be:

1. To trust in any form of organization, or in any spiritual gift or configuration of gifts, or in any gifted person's ministry, to bring new life to a church is indeed Spirit-quenching. When hope rests on these factors rather than on God, prayer fades, pride blossoms, and God's blessing is withheld.

2. The old idea that spiritual ministry is the task of the clergy and some few specially zealous layfolk, while the rest limit themselves to praying, paying, and looking after the church fabric and church meals, is also Spirit-quenching in itself (though congregations have occasionally prospered despite it). The biblical principle of every-member ministry in the body of Christ must be recognized, and a place must be found in the church's life for every God-given gift to be used in God's service—which makes a certain amount of organization mandatory.

3. As in Nehemiah's project a leader's charisma, communal willingness to work for God's cause, basic building skills, and good organization harnessing them, all combined to erect Jerusalem's walls, so in our churches a leader's charisma, communal willingness to serve, ministry gifts

found and honed in the entire congregation, and good organization to make the best use of them, must all combine for true renewal. Neither the most powerful preaching nor the most exuberant display of spiritual manifestations will build up the local church without the organizational wisdom that sets goals and devises means to ends. The preaching pastors who have left behind them the most virile and mature churches have been those whose pulpit work was linked with good organizing, done by others if not by themselves. Check it out: you will find that it is so.

CHAPTER FOUR

Man-Management II: Keeping Going

G etting the work on the wall started was a major achievement, but keeping it going proved to be the tougher task.

When Sanballat heard that we were rebuilding the wall, he became angry and was greatly incensed. He ridiculed the Jews, and in the presence of his associates and the army of Samaria, he said, "What are those feeble Jews doing? Will they restore their wall? Will they offer sacrifices? Will they finish in a day? Can they bring the stones back to life from those heaps of rubble—burned as they are?"

Tobiah the Ammonite, who was at his side, said, "What they are building—if even a fox climbed up on it, he would break down their wall of stones!"

Hear us, O our God, for we are despised. Turn their insults back on their own heads. Give them over as plunder in a land of captivity. Do not cover up their guilt or blot out their sins from your sight, for they have thrown insults in the face of the builders.

So we rebuilt the wall till all of it reached half its height, for the people worked with all their heart.

But when Sanballat, Tobiah, the Arabs, the Ammonites and the men of Ashdod heard that the repairs to Jerusalem's walls had gone ahead and that the gaps were being closed, they were very angry. They all plotted together to come and fight against Jerusalem and stir up trouble against it. But we prayed to our God and posted a guard day and night to meet this threat.

Meanwhile, the people in Judah said, "The strength of the laborers is giving out, and there is so much rubble that we cannot rebuild the wall."

Also our enemies said, "Before they know it or see us, we will be right there among them and will kill them and put an end to the work."

Then the Jews who lived near them came and told us ten times over, "Wherever you turn, they will attack us."

Therefore I stationed some of the people behind the lowest points of the wall at the exposed places, posting them by families, with their swords, spears and bows. After I looked things over, I stood up and said to the nobles, the officials and the rest of the people, "Don't be afraid of them. Remember the Lord, who is great and awesome, and fight for your brothers, your sons and your daughters, your wives and your homes."

When our enemies heard that we were aware of their plot and that God had frustrated it, we all returned to the wall, each to his own work.

From that day on, half of my men did the work, while the other half were equipped with spears, shields, bows and armor. The officers posted themselves behind all the people of Judah who were building the wall. Those who carried materials did their work with one hand and held a weapon in the other, and each of the builders wore his sword at his side as he worked. But the man who sounded the trumpet stayed with me.

Then I said to the nobles, the officials and the rest of

the people, "The work is extensive and spread out, and we are widely separated from each other along the wall. Wherever you hear the sound of the trumpet, join us there. Our God will fight for us!"

So we continued the work with half the men holding spears, from the first light of dawn till the stars came out. At that time I also said to the people, "Have every man and his helper stay inside Jerusalem at night, so they can serve us as guards by night and workmen by day." Neither I nor my brothers nor my men nor the guards with me took off our clothes; each had his weapon, even when he went for water.

(Nehemiah 4:1-23)

SATAN

The real theme of Nehemiah 4–6 is spiritual warfare, and Nehemiah's real opponent, lurking behind the human opponents, critics, and grumblers who occupied his attention directly, was Satan, whose name means "adversary" and who operates as the permanent enemy of God, God's people, God's work, and God's praise. Nehemiah does not mention him (few Old Testament books do), but that does not mean that he was not there. Direct opposition on the human level to those who are obeying God, and the use of "flaming arrows" of discouragement (Eph. 6:16) to destroy hope, induce fear, and so paralyze their endeavors, are two of his regular tactics, and both are in evidence in these chapters. When you see Satan's fingerprints on events, it is a safe bet that Satan himself is actively present, even if he carefully keeps himself out of sight.

We think of Satan as our spiritual enemy, and so he is, but we need to realize that the reason he hates humankind and seeks our ruin is because he hates God, his and our Creator. He is not a creator himself, only a destroyer; he is a fallen angel, the archetypal instance of good gone wrong; and now he seeks only to thwart God's plans, wreck his work, rob him of glory, and in that sense triumph over him. When God initiates something for his praise, Satan is always there, trying to keep pace with him, planning ways of spoiling and frustrating the divine project. "Devil," his descriptive title, means "slanderer," one who thinks, speaks, and plans evil, first against God himself, secondarily against the human race. The army of bodiless intelligences that the Gospels call demons has "as king over them the angel of the Abyss, whose name in Hebrew is Abaddon, and in Greek, Apollyon" (Rev. 9:11)—both names meaning "destroyer." For his fierce, sustained, pitiless hatred of humanity Satan is spoken of as a murderer, the evil one, a roaring and devouring lion, and a great red dragon. For his habit of twisting truth as a means to his ends he is called a liar and a deceiver. He is malicious, mean, ugly, and cruel to the last degree.

A reckless and contemptuous boredom with Christianity leads some today, as in former days, to flirt with Satanism for kicks, but this is in truth suicidal folly, for the Satan of Scripture hates and seeks to fool all mankind, those who claim allegiance to him no less than others. Also, he is extremely cunning, much cleverer than we are, and is highly skilled at manipulating and using people to bring about his destructive goals. (Think of Eve, whom Satan deceived [2 Cor. 11:3; 1 Tim. 2:14], and of Judas, into whom Satan entered to prompt treason and apostasy [Jn. 13:27], and of Elymas, occultist and foe of the faith, to whom Paul needed to say, "You are a child of the devil . . . will you never stop perverting the right ways of the Lord?" [Acts 13:10].) Altogether, the devil is an enemy who has to be taken very seriously.

Yet we should not panic in the face of his attentions. Christ has overcome him (Jn. 12:31); Satan is now a defeated foe, a lion on a chain, and what he can do against

us is sovereignly restricted on a day-to-day basis, for "God
. . . will not let you be tempted beyond what you can bear"
(1 Cor. 10:13). We who are Christ's should detest Satan but
not dread him, since God now provides us with all-purpose
combat equipment for use against him. It is the Christian's
privilege to "put on the full armor of God, so that when the
day of evil comes, you may be able to stand your ground"
(Eph. 6:13). Running scared of Satan is not the Christian
way; it is, rather, an expression of unbelief. Wisdom directs,
not that we should spend our time worrying about Satan,
as if there is no limit to what he can do, but simply that we
should watch for signs of his being on the move—that is,
for actions, passions, and circumstances that make war
against the cause and the honor of the Creator. Such events
call for precisely the reaction of prayer and countermoves
that we see in Nehemiah. Nehemiah's battles as the wall
went up can teach us much about winning our bit of the
war into which, with Nehemiah, we who seek to serve God
have walked.

SATAN'S MEN

In describing his conflicts, Nehemiah focuses on three leaders of the opposition: Sanballat, Tobiah, and Geshem. He
tells us that the first two "were very much disturbed that
someone had come to promote the welfare of the Israelites"
(2:10); that he informed them at the outset they had "no
share in Jerusalem or any claim or historic right to it" (2:20);
that all three "mocked and ridiculed" the enterprise of
rebuilding and accused its promoters of "rebelling against
the [Persian] king" (2:19; 6:5-7); that Sanballat made a contemptuous anti-Jewish speech, and Tobiah a feeble anti-
Jewish joke, at a rally of their associates in government plus
the Samaritan army, where they poured public scorn on the
whole undertaking; that in face of its progress they with

some other groups "were very angry" and "plotted together to come and fight against Jerusalem" (4:7-8); and that when the wall was finished and only the gates needed to be set in place, the three ringleaders made a final flurry of attempts to intimidate, incriminate, and even assassinate Nehemiah (6:1-14, 17-19; see especially vv. 2, 13, 14, 19). What are we to make of these angry men who became Satan's tools in opposing Jerusalem's restoration?

Personal details first. Sanballat's name is Babylonian. Nehemiah calls him a Horonite (2:10, 19; 13:28)—that is, a native of Beth-Horon, eighteen miles northwest of Jerusalem—and reports that many years later his daughter married into the high priest's family (13:28). Extrabiblical sources tell us that he was the elderly governor of Samaria in 407 B.C., thirty-eight years after Nehemiah came to Jerusalem and built the wall, and that his two sons bore Jewish names that celebrated Yahweh. The natural guess is that Sanballat was a non-Jew, though perhaps married to a Jewish woman, that he had already become governor of Samaria before Nehemiah arrived, that he had no religious interest or motivation of any kind, and that he was very anxious to carve out a career by showing himself a loyal servant of the Persian regime; also, he was very fearful lest he jeopardize his prospects and forfeit his ambition by letting seeds of revolt be sown on his own doorstep.

He was, then, a thoroughly worldly man who opposed Nehemiah in order to keep his nose clean with his Persian masters and also, no doubt, to avoid the destabilizing emergence of a new power base less than forty miles from his own headquarters. No doubt he was quite sincere in ascribing to Nehemiah and his colleagues a secret purpose of rebellion, which they would naturally not announce till they thought they were strong enough to carry it out.

Pleasure, profit, and power are the only motivating allurements that worldlings understand, and we can imagine

Sanballat pontifically explaining to his friends that since there was clearly no pleasure in this back-breaking construction job that Nehemiah had taken on, his goal must by elimination be profit or power or both. Worldlings today accuse Christians of the same self-serving purposes; there is nothing new under the sun. The honor and praise of God as a motive for action clearly meant nothing to Sanballat, and in this he is typical of fallen mankind generally.

Tobiah ("Yahweh is good") is a Jewish name, and its bearer had married into an influential Jewish family that gave him personal links with some of Jerusalem's top people, including Eliashib the high priest, whose son had married Sanballat's daughter (6:17-19; 13:4-5). Tobiah's son, too, had married into Israel's aristocracy. Evidently the top people regarded Tobiah as one of themselves and resented Nehemiah's negative attitude to him (see 6:17-19). Yet Tobiah, "the Ammonite official" (2:10)—that is, the Jew who had made Ammon "his chosen sphere, in which he had gained high office"[1]—had ganged up with Sanballat in regretting, scorning, and opposing the reconstruction of Jerusalem's walls. He, too, it seems, was a careerist in Persian employ, perhaps already governor of Ammon, or if not, hoping soon to be, and not willing to risk his position and prospects by sanctioning a project that to his mind could only cause trouble. He was a worldly-wise formalist and pragmatist, hard-hearted as well as hard-headed, who was not so foolish as to let his faith affect his personal or professional life. To him also the glory of God as a motive meant precisely nothing. He was a cynic, of a kind quite familiar in the modern world.

What of "Geshem the Arab" (2:19)? Writes Kidner: "There is evidence that Geshem (cf. 6:1 ff.), far from being a negligible alien, was an even more powerful figure than his companions. . . . From other sources it emerges that Geshem and his son ruled a league of Arabian tribes which took control of Moab and Edom (Judah's neighbours to the east and south) together with part of Arabia and approaches to Egypt, under the Persian Empire."[2] He was clearly a sort of paramount chief, but that did not make him more than a large-scale, diplomatically attuned power broker, and he was of course a pagan. It is sad that he, Sanballat, and Tobiah should have become, or at least tried to become, a political threesome pledged to stop God from being glorified in Jerusalem.

Sometimes in the secular world where Christian groups seek freedom to act out their faith in its fullness, and sometimes in the half-secular world of mainline denominational life as it is today, Sanballat, Tobiah, and Geshem reappear. They take the form of bureaucrats who see any version of Christianity that challenges the status quo as subversive: unnecessary, unwise, and destructive rather than constructive in its thrust. In local churches and parachurch bodies, any leader who values order above ardor and routine above revival, and who pours cold water on visionaries as soon as they propose that something be done, risks becoming a new Sanballat or Tobiah. The loyalty of such people, whereby they think they serve God, is given to Christian institutions rather than to biblical truth, and they have no idea that in this they become Satan's tools for the snuffing out of spiritual life; nor do they ever understand why Christians who have learned their faith and calling from the Bible find it necessary to fight them. The pride reflected in their confidence that wisdom is with them, and that they have a Christian duty to uphold the status quo against Bible-based reformers, makes the Sanballats and Tobiahs of our time into figures who are pathetic and tragic at the same time. But that does not in any way reduce our obligation to stand against them when they oppose obedience to God's truth. Nehemiah is our model here, a very relevant model for our time.

PSYCHOLOGICAL WARFARE

We turn now to the three types of attack that Satan used his human agents to mount against Nehemiah's great team of builders. There was psychological warfare, there were physical threats, and there were personal discouragements and underminings. Chapter 4 of Nehemiah's book shows all three. We will take them in order.

Psychological warfare, as we nowadays call it, is concerned with the destroying of morale. Mockery and contempt, whereby you show that you regard me as a pig-headed fool, is a very telling weapon for the purpose. Morale is challenged at the deepest level when we find that others are making fun of us and telling each other how utterly stupid we are to be doing what we are doing. Sanballat in his anger understood this and proceeded to act accordingly. Whether he held his rally within earshot of Jerusalem, as some suppose, or whether he arranged for persons who were present at it to go straight to Jerusalem and spread the word about what had been said, we do not know. All we know is what Nehemiah tells us—namely, that news of what Sanballat and Tobiah had said actually got through. Each of Sanballat's rhetorical questions (the key points of his speech, obviously) is a puncturing jab at the builders' morale. Nehemiah under God had generated exhilaration, the sense that reconstruction was possible after all and that the forty-one teams by pulling together would be able to make it happen. Sanballat was resolved to generate depression and hopelessness and planned his speech to his supporters (4:2) accordingly.

"What are those feeble Jews doing?" (See what a poor incompetent lot they really are!) "Will they restore their wall?" (The task is certainly beyond them.) "Will they offer sacrifices?" —that is, do they imagine that some extra devotional exercises will cause the walls to rise as if by magic?

(What an absurd idea!) "Will they finish in a day?"—that is, do they realize what an enormous task they have taken on, and how long it is likely to take them? (It's dollars to doughnuts that they aren't in the least realistic about that!) "Can they bring the stones back to life from those heaps of rubble—burned as they are?" (Don't they know that burned stones crumble?) In fact, it was only the gates of the city that had been burned, and the walls as such had simply been thrown down; so most of the stones had not been calcined and thus could be used again. No doubt, however, the point went down well with Sanballat's rally crowd, who by then were in a mood to accept even Tobiah's leaden witticism ("if a fox climbed their wall, it would collapse!") as if it was a word of wisdom (4:3). "Even from a man of importance, so fatuous a joke needs a little help from the atmosphere," comments Kidner drily,[3] and of course he is right.

Nehemiah's response to this opening salvo in the war of nerves is striking. With careful calculation Sanballat had played on the inner insecurity, self-doubt, and fear of failing that in this fallen world are part of most people's makeup, and that experience must have been brought to epic proportions in the hangdog Jerusalemites. Sanballat's purpose was to paralyze effort by inducing hopelessness and despair, and Nehemiah must have realized that he might very easily succeed. Morale, though high, was fragile, and it would not take much to lower it.

Nor should we suppose that Nehemiah himself was immune to the impact of what Sanballat was saying: no one knew better than he that the Jews were indeed feeble, that the task was huge, that there was no magic formula for success, that it might well prove to be a very long job, and that reusing stones picked out of the rubble of a wall demolished some time before would be a tricky and depressing business, without any of the romance involved in building a new structure out of new materials. No one is a leader any longer

than people actually follow him; should the workers conclude that the task was impossible and give it up, Nehemiah
would still be governor, but his leadership would be at an
end. So, driven as much by his own renewed anxieties as by
his months-old purpose of raising the wall again to the glory
of God, he went once more to prayer. As we have seen
already, Nehemiah wants to underline the fact that all he did
was accomplished through prayer; so we need not be surprised at his abrupt insertion of the substance of his praying
at that time (4:4-5).

His prayer crystallizes into a twofold plea, thus:

1. *A plea for God's support of his own servants.* That is the
meaning of: "Hear us, O our God, for we are despised . . .
they have thrown insults in the face of the builders."
Nehemiah is asking God to counter the weakening effect of
Sanballat's words by imparting fresh strength and confidence to the working teams.

2. *A plea for God's judgment on his own enemies.* That is the
meaning of: "Turn their insults back on their own heads. . . .
Do not cover up their guilt or blot out their sins from your
sight." Nehemiah is not expressing personal vindictiveness
against Sanballat and Tobiah so much as zeal for God to vindicate himself against them because they have opposed him.
The same is true of the various imprecatory Psalms, in which
the God of justice is asked to reverse situations in which
might has seemed to be right and crime seems to have paid.
Here, too, the longing that for his own praise God would
deal with the ungodly as they deserve is central.

Difficulty is felt today with biblical prayers that God will
take vengeance, partly because of their oriental exuberance of
expression, which to us sounds like bloodthirstiness and
gloating (imaginative detail about anyone's evil prospects is
culturally unacceptable to Westerners), but mainly because
the pure zeal for God's glory that these prayers express is foreign to our spiritually sluggish hearts. The key principle here

is stated in Psalm 139:21-22: "Do I not hate those who hate you, O Lord . . . ? I have nothing but hatred for them; I count them my enemies." The nearer we come to this state of mind, which is a spinoff from the desire that God's will be done, his kingdom come, and his name be hallowed and glorified, the less problem shall we have with vengeance prayers.

Sometimes it is said that such praying is an Old Testament phenomenon that the New Testament leaves behind and even implicitly condemns, but this is not so. In the book of the Revelation the martyrs cry, "How long, Sovereign Lord, holy and true, until you judge the inhabitants of the earth and avenge our blood?" (6:10); and when finally Babylon, emblem of the world's pride, greed, callousness, and cruelty, is overthrown, saints and angels join in singing, "Hallelujah! Salvation and glory and power belong to our God, for true and just are his judgments. . . . Hallelujah! The smoke from her goes up for ever and ever" (19:1-3). What we are being shown here is that when Christians get to heaven, with their sanctification complete and their minds as fully conformed to the mind of Christ as the angels' minds are, they will forever rejoice not only in the mercies by which God has glorified himself in their own lives, but also in the judgments by which he vindicates himself against those who defy him. Christians sometimes find this hard to believe because, being at present imperfectly sanctified sinners themselves, they have so much fellow-feeling for other sinners, and as yet so little sense of how God is glorified in his retributive judgments. But there can be no doubt that learning to praise God properly for his judgments, no less than for his mercies, is something that all the saints have to look forward to, as part of God's schooling of them in the life of holiness.

"Love your enemies . . . pray for those who mistreat you," said Jesus (Lk. 6:27-28), and the desire that the love and the prayer must express is that God should show mercy on our enemies by fully converting them to himself. Jesus modeled this unforgettably when he prayed for the soldiers who nailed him to the cross: "Father, forgive them, for they do not know what they are doing" (Lk. 23:34). His reference to his prayers for Jerusalem—"how often I have longed to gather your children together, as a hen gathers her chicks under her wings" (Mt. 23:37)—tells the same story. Yet Jesus also spoke matter-of-factly, and with no indication of distress, about the day when he himself would justly banish from his presence to endless misery persons who had not truly given him their heart (Mt. 7:23; 10:33; 23:33-35; 24:48-51; 25:41-46; etc.). So too Paul spoke matter-of-factly about the judgment ("the wrath of God") that was upon the Jews, for whose conversion he earnestly prayed (see Rom. 10:1; 1 Thess. 2:14-16).

The truth is that restraining the desire for revenge and asking God to show mercy to *your* enemies by converting them, while at the same time you acknowledge that he will certainly judge *his* enemies, and even asking him to start doing that at once, are not mutually exclusive lines of prayer. Both are expressions of God-glorifying desire, both have the hallowing of God's name as their goal, and of necessity we express both in major ignorance of the details of God's plan as it relates to the destinies of individuals. But Scripture shows us very plainly that petitionary prayer, expressing the desire that God's will be done, is itself an activity that God wills, and further that we cannot expect him to do anything that we hope for if we have not explicitly asked him to; and that knowledge should suffice to keep us praying both for the conversion of people we know and for the overthrow of all who oppose the work of God.

Did Nehemiah ever pray for the conversion of Sanballat and Tobiah? We do not know. Perhaps he did not, and perhaps he would have been a better man if he had done so (as was said earlier, there is no reason to think

Nehemiah was sinless, or to deny that in his zeal for God's glory he was inclined to be harsh and narrow). But since Sanballat and Tobiah actually opposed him all along, and thereby actually opposed God, it is naturally his prayers against their continuing influence, and his commitment of them to God to deal with, that he records.

And certainly the thing Nehemiah wants his readers to know is that this prayer for upholding in face of the attempted undermining was answered in a very decisive way. Morale held steady, and whatever anger Sanballat and Tobiah had generated by their scoffing remarks served only to energize the labor gangs. ("Is that what they think? We'll show them!") "So we rebuilt the wall till all of it reached half its height, for the people worked with all their heart" (4:6). Thus the first form of opposition, psychological pressure, was overcome.

PHYSICAL THREATS

Threats of an invasion to demolish what had been built thus far was the next problem. Ill-wishers to the rebuilding enterprise lived all around the city, and Sanballat in Samaria to the north, Tobiah and the Ammonites on the east side, plus Arabs to the south and the forces of Ashdod to the west "all plotted together to come and fight against Jerusalem" (4:8). Very discouraging news! The combined forces surrounding the holy city were bound to be numerically superior, and the message that came through was that they were sure of their ability to launch an effective surprise attack—"Before they know it or see us, we will be right there among them and will kill them and put an end to the work" (4:11).

The message came, it seems, via Jews who lived "near them" (v. 12)—Jewish settlers and homesteaders, that is, on something like a thirty-mile radius around Jerusalem, living close to the centers of hostile activity. As backers of the rebuilding, these rural Jews sorrowfully "came and told us ten times over, 'Wherever you turn, they will attack us'" (4:12). Told "*us*," not *me*, writes Nehemiah; evidently the visitors from the countryside gossiped to all and sundry about the gatherings of troops and the stockpiling of arms. From the fact that they said the invaders would attack "*us*" it is clear that they saw themselves as supporters; but for all that, their gloomy gossiping was well calculated to disrupt the work by spreading alarm and despondency on a grand scale. With friends like this, Nehemiah must have thought, who needs enemies? Though the rural Jews obviously thought they were being helpful by saying what they said, and had apparently made special journeys for the purpose, their assurance that there was no way of avoiding attack could not but depress and demoralize, and Nehemiah's "ten times" (as we might say, "if he told me once, he told me a dozen times") shows something of his irritation. Pontifications about overwhelming forces lined up against Jerusalem, with warnings that resistance would be hopeless, were the last thing that he and the builders needed, just as declarations that nothing can be done to move the churches forward are the last thing that pastors and congregational leaders need to hear today. But as it was in the days of Nehemiah, so it continues to be: few if any churches lack friends, of a sort, who feel it is their special ministry to impart negative assurances of this kind, and who never doubt that their doomsaying is the most helpful contribution they can make. The factual information they bring may, of course, be useful; but the oracular gloom they spread is unbelief masquerading as wisdom and needs to be nipped in the bud.

Nehemiah, as we have seen, was a practical embodiment of William Carey's noble dictum, "Attempt great things for God—expect great things from God"; and he was not prepared to throw in the towel just yet. James Montgomery Boice writes well about Nehemiah's next move:

> In military terms, Nehemiah must have known it was unlikely that his enemies would attack the city in full force, since he had the imposing authority of Artaxerxes behind him.. . . . On the other hand, Nehemiah must have known that what we might call guerrilla warfare was likely. . . . Besides, he knew that anything of this nature would so demoralize the people that the work would stop and would never get going again. What was Nehemiah to do? What he did was extremely wise. He dealt with the real threat . . . in a way that built the people's low self-esteem and strengthened their resolve.
>
> Nehemiah turned Jerusalem into an armed camp.
>
> When the threat became known, he responded by posting a guard day and night (v. 9). When the rumors of violence continued and began to have a demoralizing effect, he went further: (1) he stopped the work (cp. vv. 13, 15); (2) he armed the people (v. 13 [vv. 17, 18, also]); and (3) he arranged the people in family groups at the most exposed places along the wall (v. 13). Dividing them into families corresponded with Israel's traditional way of fighting and heightened each person's awareness of the stakes. . . .
>
> When his enemies learned of the Jews' preparation and that their plot [the surprise attack] was frustrated, the pressure lessened and Nehemiah was able to return the workers to the walls. But he did not forget the threat. Therefore, (1) he divided the people into two groups, one of which would work and the other which would be in readiness to fight at any time (. . . vv. 16-18); (2) he devised a plan for meeting an unexpected attack (vv. 18-20); (3) he accelerated the pace of the building (from dawn until the stars came out (v. 21); and (4) he kept the people in the city day and night (v. 23).[4]

Nor was this all. Nehemiah did three further things that may well have contributed more to the long-term success of the building project than any of his masterful strokes as an organizer. First, he kept the people in good heart by constantly sharing with them his own total trust and confidence in God. "Don't be afraid of them. Remember the Lord, who is great and awesome, and fight . . ." "Our God will fight for us!" (4:14, 20). In this way he was a constant inspiration and morale-booster, and that was a ministry of incalculable significance.

Second, from the beginning of the crisis Nehemiah was praying explicitly for God's protection and stirring others up to join with him in this. "*We* [the entire community] prayed to our God" (v. 9)—and throughout the crisis continued to do so. Prayer moves mountains, said Jesus (Mt. 17:20; Mk. 11:23); no limits can be set to the difference that faithful praying makes in times of trouble.

Third, Nehemiah accepted for himself the hardships that he imposed on the people during the emergency. "Neither I nor my brothers nor my men nor the guards with me took off our clothes; each had his weapon . . ." (4:23). This is how leaders build loyalty among those they lead, fostering among them the resolve to stay and toil together until the job is done. Understandably, it is when people see their leader identifying most closely with themselves that they identify most closely with him.

So the invasion threat was coped with in a way that actually left the people's solidarity under Nehemiah stronger than before.

PERSONAL DISCOURAGEMENT

Coping with the danger of hostile military action had made the task of rebuilding more complicated, and a good deal harder. The need for Nehemiah to detach "half" of his men from the work force to serve as a fully armed guard (4:16), and the awkwardness of every builder having to wear a sword and every fetcher and carrier having to hold a spear while struggling with spades, stones, and mortar (4:18) inevitably slowed things down and imposed extra burdens that nobody had bargained for. Nor was that all. While the defense crisis was escalating, "the people in Judah said, 'The strength of the laborers is giving out, and there is so much rubble that we cannot rebuild the wall'" (4:10). The exhilaration with which they had embraced the task of rebuilding had not been fully realistic. The clearing of the rubble from the past so that the new walls could be given proper foundations was proving to be a much larger job than they had thought, and the builders, faced with perhaps twice as much work as they had anticipated, were losing heart. Nehemiah had to deal with the defense problem knowing that more and more of the workers on his teams were coming to suspect that, even without threats from outside, the job was simply beyond them and they could never hope to complete it. Personal discouragement at the magnitude of their assigned tasks, discouragement of the kind that drains away enterprise, diminishes effort, and generates the apathy and inertia of hopelessness, was rapidly infecting the whole work force. This, too, was Nehemiah's problem.

And not Nehemiah's only. Pastors and spiritual leaders today whose concerns extend beyond maintenance to mission, and who seek a genuine extending of God's kingdom, find themselves faced again and again with what has to be classed as attitudinal rubble—laziness, unbelief, procrastination, cynicism, self-absorption, in-fighting and fence-sitting among the Lord's people, and many similar factors that hinder and obstruct spiritual advance. These make the task of leadership twice as hard as it would otherwise be, and the going twice as slow. Nehemiah himself, facing ridicule from Sanballat and Tobiah and their friends, plus the threat of guerrilla infiltration to level the walls once more, plus now the builders' despairing complaints, must have felt the temptation to give up hope as strongly as did any of those he led, just as Moses must have felt it many times at the people's folly in the wilderness wanderings, and Paul over and over at the inroads of heresy, immaturity, and immorality in the churches he planted, and Jesus again and again at the spiritual dullness of his own closest disciples. Yet they all kept going, just as true spiritual leaders today will keep going despite misunderstanding, malice, and hostility in all its forms. For there is a secret source of strength on which leaders, like their followers, may always draw, both to stabilize and re-encourage themselves and to equip themselves to re-encourage others.

What source is this? Nehemiah's admonition— "Remember the Lord"—has already pointed us to it. The source of strength is the knowledge of God, recalled, reviewed, refocused, thought through, and applied to the matters in hand. The God we serve is, as Nehemiah declared, "great and awesome;" "great" in his wisdom, grace, faithfulness, and power, and "awesome" in his habit of exposing his servants to difficulties, dangers, toils, and snares out of which he then delivers them. To be a fellow-laborer with this God and share in his works of love, blessing, and redemption in this world is a marvelous privilege, the greatest that life affords. The work may be tougher than we bargained for, but we should still feel the awe and the glory of being God's colleague. And never forget that, as someone once said, one with God is a majority, or that, as someone else has said, while the wages for serving God here may be scrappy, the pension is out of this world. Nehemiah knew these things, and so was able both to face opposition as a good swimmer faces the waves and to speak words that put new hope into his flagging and faint-hearted followers. "Wherever you hear the sound of the trumpet, join us there. Our God will fight for us!" (4:20). "The God of heaven will give us success" (2:20). As Nehemiah's declarations expressed conviction, so they brought conviction;

Jerusalem rallied to resist invasion, and the clearing of the rubble was resumed. Discouragement, one of Satan's strongest weapons, was thus effectively countered. By the grace of God, and in the strength of God, the work of God went on.

"If you can keep your head while all around you / Are losing theirs, and blaming it on you . . . you'll be a Man, my son," wrote Kipling. Nehemiah, like Moses, Paul, and Jesus, showed himself to be a Man in Kipling's sense, and perhaps in a profounder sense than Kipling ever understood. It is those who know their God who are able to keep their head in panicky conditions, and they can do this because of what is in their heart. What is that? Not just an intellectual ortho-doxy, but an unflagging, all-absorbing passion for closeness to God himself. Only this explains the sense of God's power that radiates from their lives, the steadying shrewdness of the things they say, and their gift for imparting new hope to those who have lost hope. Whether Nehemiah fed his soul on David's Psalms is more than we know (he might have done so); but certainly David is most vivid in voicing the thoughts of the heart that is rooted in God and that must have constituted Nehemiah's inner profile, and David shall have the last word in this chapter on how God's servants keep going.

> The LORD is my light and my salvation—
> whom shall I fear?
> The LORD is the stronghold of my life—
> of whom shall I be afraid?
> When evil men advance against me to devour my flesh,
> when my enemies and my foes attack me,
> they will stumble and fall.
> Though an army besiege me, my heart will not fear;
> though war break out against me,
> even then will I be confident.

One thing I ask of the LORD,
this is what I seek:
> *that I may dwell in the house of the LORD all the*
> *days of my life,*
> *to gaze upon the beauty of the LORD and to seek*
> *him in his temple.*

Teach me your way, O LORD,
lead me in a straight path because of my oppressors.

Wait for the LORD,
be strong and take heart and wait for the LORD.

(Ps. 27:1-4, 11, 14)

CHAPTER FIVE

Tested for Destruction

Forty years ago Nevil Shute was Britain's best-selling popular novelist, and deservedly so. An aeronautical engineer by training, he moved through spare-time thriller-writing into a fascinating series of human-interest stories in which he explored very vividly aspects of un-self-conscious decency in the common man—integrity, loyalty, love, courage, fidelity, honesty, responsibility, and quiet, self-denying heroism in everyday life. The stories appealed because they were sparked by contemporary events and faced up to real-life problems in thoughtful and sometimes devastating ways. *No Highway* was, I think, the first Shute I read, and it is certainly the one I best remember. It tells of a department head who risks his career by supporting an eccentric researcher who believes that the tailplane of a passenger aircraft then in service would break off through metal fatigue after so many hours of flying. All through the story one such tailplane is being tested to destruction, and the climax of the book includes its disintegration at approximately the predicted time. The story still gives me the shivers, partly for its picture of professionals willing to suppress theorists and to endanger people rather than blow a warning whistle; partly for its reminder of the dilemmas that knowledge with integrity can generate; partly, I guess, because I recall how one of Britain's first jets, a Comet, did in fact spectacularly come apart in mid-air through metal fatigue, killing among others the then-director of the Overseas Missionary Fellowship, with whom I had a small personal link; and partly, I know, because Shute's tale makes me think of Satan, with whom testing for destruction is every day's work.

SATAN'S STRATEGY

Scripture, as we saw, speaks of both God and Satan "tempting"—that is, trying people out to see what is in them, testing them as students are tested in school examinations. We read that Jesus was tempted by the devil (Mt. 4:1), and that God tempted Abraham (Gen. 22:1, KJV), and the truth is that in every testing situation both Satan and God are involved. God tests us to bring forth excellence in discipleship, as Moses explained to the Israelites at the close of the wilderness wanderings: "Remember how the LORD your God led you all the way in the desert these forty years, to humble you and to *test* you in order to know what was in your heart, whether or not you would keep his commands. . . . He gave you manna . . . to humble and to *test* you"—to drill you, that is, in grateful, confident, disciplined, submissive reliance on himself—"so that in the end it might go well with you" (Dt. 8:2, 16). Satan, by contrast, tests us with a view to our ruin and destruction, as appears from Paul's reason for sending Timothy to strengthen and encourage the harassed Thessalonian Christians: "I was afraid that in some way the tempter might have *tempted* you and our efforts might have been useless"— in other words, Satan might have persuaded them to give up their faith and so ruined their souls (1 Thess. 3:2-5).

Satan was, of course, with the Israelites in the desert, laboring to ensnare them in unbelief and lawlessness of various kinds, and often succeeding in his purpose, in the short term at least; and God was with the Thessalonians in the furnace, disciplining them for their good, that they might share his holiness (see Heb. 12:10). Temptation is always two-sided in this way; so whenever we are conscious of Satan seeking to pull us down, we should remind ourselves that God is present too to keep us steady and to build us up through the harrowing experience. That is something we must never forget.

But Satan is a hater, a wrecker, and a destroyer, and only when he is ruining God's work in individuals and communities is he happy. Earlier I suggested that Nehemiah's narrative of opposition to the building of the walls should be understood in terms of Satan's hidden hand of hatred to the work of God, and in the present chapter we shall follow that clue further. In Nehemiah 4 we saw Satan using three devices—psychological warfare, physical threats, and personal discouragement—to nullify Nehemiah's rebuilding project. In Nehemiah 5 and 6 we shall see him, having failed so far, turning his attention to Nehemiah in a more direct way, working to destroy him personally in the sense of so discrediting him that his role as leader of God's people in God's work would be forfeited. We shall watch Satan deploy four devices to this end: incrimination, intrigue, innuendo, and intimidation: he is nothing if not versatile! And we shall also see Nehemiah by faith, wisdom, and goodwill coping successfully with each of these forms of entrapment, right up to his first great pinnacle of achievement—the completion of the wall "in fifty-two days . . . with the help of our God"— an amazing amount of work to have got through within a two-month period, and a troubled one at that (6:15-16). We shall find it to be a story of spiritual warfare and spiritual tri-

umph, full of lessons and encouragements for every servant
of God.

Satan's opening ploy was subtle. It began with a generating of grievances that threatened to stop the work; that it
was also an attempt to besmirch Nehemiah and alienate him
from the community as a whole only became clear later. This
is how Nehemiah narrates what took place.

> Now the men and their wives raised a great outcry
> against their Jewish brothers. Some were saying, "We
> and our sons and daughters are numerous; in order for
> us to eat and stay alive, we must get grain."
>
> Others were saying, "We are mortgaging our fields,
> our vineyards and our homes to get grain during the
> famine."
>
> Still others were saying, "We have had to borrow
> money to pay the king's tax on our fields and vineyards.
> Although we are of the same flesh and blood as our
> countrymen and though our sons are as good as theirs,
> yet we have to subject our sons and daughters to slav-
> ery. Some of our daughters have already been enslaved,
> but we are powerless, because our fields and our vine-
> yards belong to others."
>
> When I heard their outcry and these charges, I was
> very angry. I pondered them in my mind and then
> accused the nobles and officials. I told them, "You are
> exacting usury from your own countrymen!" So I called
> together a large meeting to deal with them and said: "As
> far as possible, we have bought back our Jewish broth-
> ers who were sold to the Gentiles. Now you are selling
> your brothers, only for them to be sold back to us!"
> They kept quiet, because they could find nothing to say.
>
> So I continued, "What you are doing is not right.
> Shouldn't you walk in the fear of our God to avoid the
> reproach of our Gentile enemies? I and my brothers and
> my men are also lending the people money and grain.
> But let the exacting of usury stop! Give back to them

immediately their fields, vineyards, olive groves and houses, and also the usury you are charging them—the hundredth part of the money, grain, new wine and oil."

"We will give it back," they said. "And we will not demand anything more from them. We will do as you say."

Then I summoned the priests and made the nobles and officials take an oath to do what they had promised. I also shook out the folds of my robe and said, "In this way may God shake out of his house and possessions every man who does not keep this promise. So may such a man be shaken out and emptied!"

At this the whole assembly said, "Amen," and praised the Lord. And the people did as they had promised.

Moreover, from the twentieth year of King Artaxerxes, when I was appointed to be their governor in the land of Judah, until his thirty-second year—twelve years—neither I nor my brothers ate the food allotted to the governor. But the earlier governors—those preceding me—placed a heavy burden on the people and took forty shekels of silver from them in addition to food and wine. Their assistants also lorded it over the people. But out of reverence for God I did not act like that. Instead, I devoted myself to the work on this wall. All my men were assembled there for the work; we did not acquire any land.

Furthermore, a hundred and fifty Jews and officials ate at my table, as well as those who came to us from the surrounding nations. Each day one ox, six choice sheep and some poultry were prepared for me, and every ten days an abundant supply of wine of all kinds. In spite of all this, I never demanded the food allotted to the governor, because the demands were heavy on these people.

Remember me with favor, O my God, for all I have done for these people.

(Nehemiah 5)

INCRIMINATION

The chapter falls into three parts: verses 1-5, the complaints Nehemiah heard; verses 6-13, the steps Nehemiah took; verses 14-19, the example Nehemiah set. My exposition will follow this outline.

First, *the complaints Nehemiah heard* (5:1-5). In chapter 4 the picture was of a community rallying and closing ranks under pressure; here, however, the picture is of the same community coming apart at the seams because of festering grievances among its members. We hear of "a great outcry" in which wives—homemakers and mothers—joined with their husbands in protesting the way homes and families were being threatened (5:1). It looks as if the public flare-up was sudden, although, as we shall see, the matters of grievance were longtime running sores in people's lives. A sense of corporate grievance can travel through a community like wildfire once the initial complaints have broken surface, and one imagines deputations and demonstrations appearing as if from nowhere to alert Nehemiah to this cluster of social problems that, as a new arrival, he had not yet realized was there.

We are not told exactly when this happened, but it is natural to guess that it was something like a month into the rebuilding, before the invasion threats had fully cleared, while the rubble problem was still acutely felt, and before it was possible for those on the job to feel that the end of the work was in sight. A new crisis at that time was the last thing Nehemiah needed, but under Satan's skillful orchestrating hand that was what he faced: the armed-camp conditions in the city, plus the blood, toil, tears, and sweat of the labor on the walls, had brought a variety of hostile feelings to a head, and now that they were out in the open there was nothing for it but to deal with the grievances as quickly and decisively as possible.

What was it all about? Nehemiah records three specific

levels of jeopardy, made public in three specific lines of complaint. It is most natural to suppose that most if not all the
complainers belonged to families that had originally
applauded Nehemiah's project and let their men go to work
on the walls; but now that the first flush of enthusiasm was
over they were having second thoughts, which perhaps the
wives were most forthright in putting into words. However
that may be, as stated to Nehemiah, the grievances were these:

Work on the walls was cutting out work in the fields. If
things went on as they were going, there would be no harvest next year, and then families would starve (5:3).

Famine conditions (one or more bad harvests in the
past) had already obliged some of the people to mortgage
some of their land to raise money for seed-corn (5:3). But
that meant they were already desperately near to ruin; if now
bad times continued and they were unable to make repay-
ments, there was no future for them, and soon they would
lose their land entirely.

Loss of land in the manner just described, plus the need
to pay interest on loans from other sources, had compelled
some families to sell their children into slavery, as the only
way they could now keep going (5:4-5).

The bottom line was that the rebuilding of the walls, on
top of everything else, was ruining poor people and should
therefore be abandoned; and in any case the impoverished
workers themselves would have to come off the job.

In all of this, however, as Nehemiah notes, the immediate object of hostility was not himself, but "their Jewish
brothers" (5:1, 5), the wealthy folk ("nobles and officials,"
5:7) who had lent the money, confiscated the lands, and were
now cheerfully accepting girls from poor families as slaves
and preparing to take the boys as well (5:5). The bland readiness of the rich to take advantage of the poor, on a business-
is-business basis, and to deal with them in a way that left
them poorer and unhappier than before had long provoked

resentment. It was this, basically, that was now breaking surface, and it had to be dealt with. Legally, nothing was amiss; but morally, the behavior of the well-heeled was callous exploitation in a community that God had called to live in brotherhood, by a principle of neighbor-love (see Lev. 19:18), and it is very much to Nehemiah's credit that when the facts were laid before him he was shocked and furious and resolved to do something about it (5:6-7). This takes us to the next section.

Second, *the steps Nehemiah took* (5:6-13). Nehemiah's anger at the victimizing of the poor was like the anger of the Lord Jesus at the trading in the temple—not the petulant anger of one whose personal plans were being thwarted, but an agonized sense of outrage at behavior that was ungodly in its nature and abusive of others in its effect. His anger led him to think hard (5:7a)—and prayerfully, for sure, though he does not mention this—about what he should do.

Perhaps he thought first of trying to evade the issue by telling the complainers: "Look, everyone, putting up the walls is God's priority for us all; it is so important that I cannot bother about these grievances right now, and you should not be bothering about them either." But that would have shown a heartlessness equal to that of the exploiters; it would have been a personal lapse from neighbor-love on Nehemiah's part, just as it would have been if the Samaritan in Jesus' story had decided he must do some other things first before helping the Jew in the gutter. It would certainly have alienated poor people from Nehemiah's leadership, making him seem unsympathetic to their plight, and might well have led many of his work force to withdraw from the walls for good. And it would have been a failure of leadership as such, for real leaders accept responsibility for the welfare of those they lead, and no leader worth the name ever turns a blind eye to victimization. So that course of action would not do.

There was really only one option—namely, to take the bull by the horns, and this Nehemiah did. He accused the wealthy to their face of "exacting usury from your own countrymen" (5:7)—that is, arranging things for the sole purpose of making money out of them (commentators and translators hem and haw here, but this is clearly the heart of the meaning)—and, said Nehemiah, that has got to stop. He formally indicted these moneymen at a public meeting that he required them to attend (5:7b-8). There he made a speech that said two things, as follows:

First, the financial dealings of the wealthy with their compatriots were anti-social, inhumane, against public policy, and for all these reasons dishonoring to God. Many Jews over the years had been sold as slaves to non-Jews, and since Nehemiah arrived as governor action had been initiated to recover and repatriate them. "As far as possible, we have bought back our Jewish brothers who were sold to the Gentiles" (5:8). The nobles, however, were still busy in the slave trade, presumably selling persons who had been put in pawn to them for slavery by bankrupt families in the manner already described. "Now you are selling your brothers, only for them to be sold back to us!" (5:8)—in other words, repurchased at public expense, no doubt through taxes raised for the purpose; thus the slave trade, which made the rich richer, was making the community poorer. Non-Jews, both those who purchased slaves from the nobles and those who did not, knew that Jews, being called to brotherhood as members of a single family, were not supposed to sell each other into slavery; it was a very bad witness, calculated to induce ridicule and contempt, and thus to dishonor Israel's divine Lord. "What you are doing is not right. Shouldn't you walk in the fear of our God to avoid the reproach of our Gentile enemies?" (5:9)—people like Sanballat and Geshem, for starters. To all of this there was, of course, no answer;

therefore, the moneymen "kept quiet" (5:8) while
Nehemiah unfolded their shortcomings.

Second, the impoverishing of the already poor must
cease and must be replaced by positive brotherly generosity.
"Let the exacting of usury stop! Give back to them immediately their fields, vineyards, olive groves and houses, and also
the usury [interest] you are charging them—the hundredth
part [per annum? per month? we do not know, and it does
not matter] of the money, grain, new wine and oil"
(5:10-11). Charge no more interest, says Nehemiah—Jews
should not ask interest from their fellow-Jews anyway
(Dt. 23:19)—and let us have a Jubilee, here and now, in
which all mortgaged and confiscated property, along with all
improperly exacted interest, returns to those from whom it
came (see Lev. 25:10-13, 47-54).

By now, one imagines, the crowd was cheering, and the
nobles were left with no choice but to accept formally and
on oath the arrangement Nehemiah had proposed (5:12).
Then Nehemiah cursed any who should break their oath,
and "the whole assembly said, 'Amen,' and praised the LORD.
And the people [the nobles and officials] did as they had
promised" (5:13). Overnight, brotherhood and help from
the rich to the poor replaced cut-throat business ethics, and
neighbor-love took the place of what Karl Marx would have
described as the class war between the proletariat and the
bourgeoisie. Once again Nehemiah's wise and masterful
leadership had saved the work of rebuilding the wall; once
again Satan was thwarted, God was honored, and his people
were blessed.

But where in all this does Satan's alleged plan to bring
Nehemiah down by incrimination come in? Rational guess-
work leads to the following hypothesis:

Satan's goal from the start was to discredit Nehemiah's
leadership and so keep the walls from being built and the
glory of God in Jerusalem from becoming a reality. To that

end, he stirred up the outcry when he did in order to impale
Nehemiah on the horns of a dilemma and to bring him
down whatever action he took. Nehemiah, faced with the
outcry, was expected to reason thus: if, on the one hand, I
ignore this scandal, or try to bypass it, my leadership will be
lost; I shall be discredited for ducking the issue. But if, on the
other hand, I move against the scandal, my leadership will
still be lost, for I shall have to admit that since coming to
Jerusalem I too have practiced usury (moneylending at interest, or at least with a requirement of collateral in some form).
No doubt Nehemiah had done this in good faith, purposing
to help people, and without fully realizing how debt situations in Jerusalem tended to escalate (after all, he had only
been there a little over a month). But the fact remained that
he had done it, and Satan expected his knowledge of having
done it to make him feel compromised and unable to take
firm action because he would thereby incriminate himself.
And no doubt Satan further expected that if knowledge of
Nehemiah's involvement in the trade of impoverishment
came out, it would in fact bring to an end his moral and spiritual leadership in the community by provoking a general
revulsion against him.

What Nehemiah actually did was both wise and brave. In
the course of his speech he frankly admitted what he had
done and immediately called for a change, implying that he
himself would be the first to make it. "I and my brothers and
my men are also lending the people money and grain. But let
the exacting of usury stop!" (5:10). Far from evoking revulsion, Nehemiah's gesture enhanced his moral credit: here
spoke an honest and good-hearted man, one who was prepared to confess his errors of judgment and lapses from wisdom and change for the better. It is perhaps understandable
that a mean creature like Satan would not expect a leader's
confession to raise his image in this way, but it did then, as it
can now. "Leaders make mistakes," writes John White. "What

marks godly leaders is the willingness to deal with mistakes openly, applying the same criterion to themselves as to others. Never shrink from doing so. You may find it embarrassing. But it is the honest road to freedom."[1] Yes, indeed.

Third, *the example Nehemiah set* (5:14-19). Here, very appropriately, as a kind of appendix to the narrative just ended, Nehemiah slips in a six-verse section showing how far from self-seeking or feathering his own nest out of the privileges and "perks" of his office he actually was. Over a period of twelve years, he tells us, he sought to follow the principle that Karl Marx was later to formulate as "from each according to his ability; to each according to his need"— which is no more, of course, than a spelling out of neighbor-love in socialist terms. Nehemiah was no socialist, but he was a philanthropist of stature, as these verses show. Throughout his governorship, writes Gordon McConville,

> he renounced the governor's food allowance, which was a tax upon the people (v. 14) . . . he refused to exploit the people (v. 15), in contrast to his predecessors . . . he acquired no land, probably highly unusual among officials of the time . . . (v. 16). It is clear that the honest policy cost Nehemiah dear. Verses 17-18 give a glimpse of the daily demands upon his hospitality, partly occasioned by his diplomatic responsibilities as governor, and partly, it seems, acceded to simply from his generosity. Nehemiah's motives in acting thus were (a) his fear of God (v. 15), which means simply that he acted out of awareness of what was appropriate for one who *worshipped* God, and (b) compassion for people's suffering (v. 18). His motives in *telling* us about it may be similar to those of the apostle Paul, who, while insisting strongly on his *right* to share in the material welfare of those among whom he worked (1 Cor. 9:8ff.), *renounced* that right lest his motivation come in question (1 Cor. 9:15).[2]

This is fair and accurate comment. Nehemiah came to Jerusalem at the call of God to improve the lot of God's people, and his mind-set throughout was that of a shepherd and a servant. He was greedy, not, as so many top people prove to be, for money, sex, and power, but for the sight of God's glory in Jerusalem, and this holy greed kept him sensitive never to seem to be on the make as it drove him to rebuild Jerusalem's walls, reestablish Jerusalem's worship, and reorder Jerusalem's life. After his initial imprudence in lending money on security in a way likely to make the poor poorer, he bent over backwards to ensure that all he and his staff did would benefit the economically depressed community that he had come to help, and as part of that purpose he conscientiously maintained his establishment with funds from other sources rather than by levying governor's taxes. Thus an impressive example of brotherliness was set by the man at the top. Recording this, Nehemiah adds the prayer that formed in his heart as he wrote—"Remember me with favor, O my God, for all I have done for these people" (5:19). He was not claiming merit but was professing sincerity in serving others for the Lord's sake. His track record entitled him to pray in these terms.

"There has always been a true elite of God's leaders," writes John White. "They are the meek who inherit the earth (Mt. 5:5). They weep and pray in secret, and defy earth and hell in public. They tremble when faced with danger, but die in their tracks rather than turn back. They are like a shepherd defending his sheep or a mother protecting her young. They sacrifice without grumbling, give without calculating, suffer without groaning. To those in their charge they say, 'We live if you do well.' Their price is above rubies. And Nehemiah was one of them." [3]

If our interpretation of chapters 5 and 6 is right, Satan did not leave Nehemiah alone after the first attempt to destroy his leadership had failed. Chapter 6 tells of three

more ploys aimed at his overthrow, involving this time the
murky triumvirate of Sanballat, Tobiah, and Geshem. Look
at Nehemiah's account of what happened next.

> When word came to Sanballat, Tobiah, Geshem the
> Arab and the rest of our enemies that I had rebuilt the
> wall and not a gap was left in it—though up to that time
> I had not set the doors in the gates—Sanballat and
> Geshem sent me this message: "Come, let us meet
> together in one of the villages on the plain of Ono."
>
> But they were scheming to harm me; so I sent mes-
> sengers to them with this reply: "I am carrying on a great
> project and cannot go down. Why should the work stop
> while I leave it and go down to you?" Four times they
> sent me the same message, and each time I gave them
> the same answer.
>
> Then, the fifth time, Sanballat sent his aide to me
> with the same message, and in his hand was an unsealed
> letter in which was written:
>
> "It is reported among the nations—and Geshem says
> it is true—that you and the Jews are plotting to revolt,
> and therefore you are building the wall. Moreover,
> according to these reports you are about to become
> their king and have even appointed prophets to make
> this proclamation about you in Jerusalem:'There is a
> king in Judah!' Now this report will get back to the king;
> so come, let us confer together."
>
> I sent him this reply: "Nothing like what you are
> saying is happening; you are just making it up out of
> your head."
>
> They were all trying to frighten us, thinking, "Their
> hands will get too weak for the work, and it will not be
> completed."
>
> But I prayed, "Now strengthen my hands."
>
> One day I went to the house of Shemaiah son of
> Delaiah, the son of Mehetabel, who was shut in at his
> home. He said, "Let us meet in the house of God, inside

the temple, and let us close the temple doors, because
men are coming to kill you—by night they are coming
to kill you."

But I said, "Should a man like me run away? Or
should one like me go into the temple to save his life? I
will not go!" I realized that God had not sent him, but
that he had prophesied against me because Tobiah and
Sanballat had hired him. He had been hired to intimidate me so that I would commit a sin by doing this, and
then they would give me a bad name to discredit me.

Remember Tobiah and Sanballat, O my God,
because of what they have done; remember also the
prophetess Noadiah and the rest of the prophets who
have been trying to intimidate me.

(Nehemiah 6:1-14)

INTRIGUE

From the standpoint of those whom Nehemiah calls "our
enemies" (6:1) the situation was now almost desperate.
Their goal all along had been to stop Jerusalem from becoming a fortified city once more, and already the walls were
complete apart from the hanging of the doors in the great
gates—a major task, no doubt, for which special scaffolding
and lifting equipment had to be set in place, and the doors
themselves specially manufactured. Sanballat and company
had only a little time, therefore, in which to frustrate the
work, and it is fascinating to watch how they used it.
Overthrowing Nehemiah personally had to be their goal, for
nothing less could stop the finishing of his project. But how
could this be done? Three ingenious ideas were tried.

Scheme 1 could be described as political softball.
Sanballat and Geshem issued a courteous, even honeyed
invitation to Nehemiah to attend a top-level consultation on
neutral ground. "Come, let us meet together in one of the

villages on the plain of Ono" (6:2)—that is, halfway between
Jerusalem and Samaria. As Dr. Boice points out, the gesture
looked like a concession speech by losers in a political campaign. "Nehemiah, it is no use pretending that we have not
been opposed to your project. We have been . . . But you have
succeeded in spite of us, and now there is no use to carry on
our opposition. For better or worse, we are going to have to
live together, you as governor of Jerusalem and ourselves as
governors of our own provinces. So let's be friends. What we
need is a summit conference. . . ."⁴ The apparent recognition
of Nehemiah's success was flattering, and the invitation to
work out a way of living together sounded advantageous and
alluring. Flattery and fancied advantage have always made a
potent combination for turning people's heads; in business
and in politics, unwary folk are having their judgment
deflected by such means all the time. But Nehemiah's head
was not turned, as his reply to the invitation shows.

"They were scheming to harm me," wrote Nehemiah.
How did he know that? Had he a spy system in place? Or
was it simply that he put two and two together—his prior
knowledge of the men inviting him and his awareness that
leopards do not change their spots, plus his sober observation that the Ono plain, a full day's journey from Jerusalem,
was on the edge of the hostile territories of Samaria and
Ashdod, and his awareness of how easily violence is arranged
in villages—and concluded, when he added up these things,
that two and two do in fact make four? No doubt he was
right to suspect an assassination plot; no doubt the sad com-
muniqué to Jerusalem—"we are very sorry to have to tell
you that there has been an unfortunate accident, and unhappily Nehemiah is dead"—had already been drafted. Four
times, however, Nehemiah refused the invitation (6:4); so
the plot came to nothing.

But note how he phrased his refusal. This was, of course,
politics, and in politics nothing impolitic that might be

quoted against you should ever be said. So Nehemiah did not refer to his suspicions of the proposers' good faith. Avoiding the language of inflammatory insult, he simply declared: "I am carrying on a great [= huge] project"—and I cannot afford the three or more days (two at least to travel, one at least to talk) that the conference would take (6:3).

Was this merely an evasive excuse? No, it was not. It was, rather, an invoking of the speaker's own true, God-given priorities. It was a wise answer, and one that revealed once more the ability to say "no" to distractions that was so marked a feature of Nehemiah's makeup. Though his ability to concentrate was partly at least, no doubt, an endowment of nature, this God-centered, goal-oriented single-mindedness was certainly sustained by grace, and Nehemiah's leadership role required it. As no amount of theory will help a would-be golfer who will not keep his eye on the ball, so no amount of wisdom will make one a leader if one cannot keep one's priorities steadily in view. Nehemiah knew from the start that God and Artaxerxes—God through Artaxerxes is how he would have put it—had sent him to Jerusalem in the first instance to rebuild its walls, and nothing was going to stand in the way of his getting that job done just as soon as possible. Such was his attitude at the outset, and it remained so as the task neared completion. And it is evident that his single-minded refusal ever to be distracted was throughout his years in Jerusalem a source of enormous strength.

John White dwells on the further point that conversations achieve little when the conversationalists' objectives diverge (as those of Nehemiah and Sanballat certainly did). White illustrates this from the days when ecumenical pressure was put on him, as president of his university Christian Union, the body affiliated to the Inter-Varsity Fellowship (now, in Britain, Universities and Colleges Christian Fellowship), to converse collaboratively, perhaps for union, with the Student Christian Movement, a body prepared to advance the proposition "That the Religions of the World Are Compatible" in public debate.[5] White's reminiscence reminded me that a generation earlier, the late Fred Crittenden, re-starter of the Oxford Inter-Collegiate Christian Union in the twenties, had been asked to converse similarly with S.C.M. leaders, perhaps to eliminate the nascent O.I.C.C.U. from the scene, and I heard him tell how he had framed his response as "O no" and used this passage in Nehemiah to warrant his refusal. Those committed to spreading a fully biblical Christianity naturally feel the echo of Nehemiah's "I am carrying on a great project" in their own hearts and have constantly found dialogue with adherents of something less to be barren and entangling. We may learn to appreciate from this standpoint also the wisdom Nehemiah showed in not taking time out for talks with Geshem and Sanballat.

INNUENDO

The fifth time Sanballat invited Nehemiah to confer at Ono, the aide who brought the invitation had with him an unsealed letter that accused the Jews of planning to rebel against Persia and to make Nehemiah their king. It ended with a threat: "Now this report will get back to the king [Artaxerxes]"— Sanballat means, I will send it to him—"so come, let us confer together" (6:6-7). This was political hardball. The *unsealed* letter would have been read many times, as indeed it was meant to be, on its journey from Samaria to Jerusalem, and the groundless but very damaging gossip that it contained was already abroad. Perhaps its contents were already on their way to Susa. There was thus more than a hint here that Nehemiah might soon need Sanballat's protection—so for that reason alone they had better talk together. The phrase "and Geshem says it is true" has been described as the Bible doctrine of rumor, and certainly it illustrates the constant character of rumor in this world; for rumors regularly cite persons of distinction as sources of information that discredits other persons of distinction or puts them on the spot, and that is exactly what we see happening in this case. Rumors spread like wildfire, for fallen human beings love to savor discreditable information about each other, and denials of rumors are not always—indeed not often—believed. What then can one do if one finds, like Nehemiah, that malicious rumors are circulating about oneself?

Nehemiah did the only two things possible: he denied the rumor in sharply matter-of-fact terms to Sanballat, its source (6:8); and he prayed, "Now strengthen my hands" (6:9). In other words, he asked God to enable him to ignore the gossip and to keep on keeping on, as inspirer, organizer, and overseer, till the rebuilding was actually completed. He recognized that the real goal of the rumor-mongering was to demoralize both himself and the people with fear of what Artaxerxes might now do if they went ahead and finished the wall, so that after all they would deliberately decide not to finish it. Therefore he prayed for extra energy to counter that fear, both in his own heart and in the hearts of the people, and to lead the builders successfully through the last lap of their task. Clearly, he resolved not to worry about his reputation, or how the king might react to Sanballat's libel (if indeed it had been sent; Sanballat, after all, might have been bluffing). These were matters beyond Nehemiah's control, which he must leave in the hands of God.

To live peacefully, work steadily, and lead vigorously despite the uncertainty of not knowing whether Artaxerxes would receive Sanballat's denunciation, and if so whether he would believe it, and if he did, whether or not he would recall Nehemiah for beheading, called for great grace. But when servants of God who find themselves in trouble humbly get on with the job God has given them to do, great grace is regularly given. One must commit one's cause to God and embrace the assurance that he will vindicate one in the end, whatever happens in the short term. Nehemiah found this to be so, and the work went on.

INTIMIDATION

Satan's third ruse against Nehemiah, arranged, as Nehemiah later discerned, through the agency of Tobiah and Sanballat, took the form of spiritual seduction—that is, an attempt to lure him through fear and the thoughtlessness fear induces into committing the sin of sacrilege. Nehemiah was summoned to the house of a professed prophet named Shemaiah, who presented to him as revelation from God an oracle that said, "men are coming to kill you—by night [tonight] they are coming to kill you." Shemaiah urged that they should both hide in the temple, where laymen like Nehemiah were not permitted to go, and where in any case no rule of sanctuary operated as it did in many pagan temples at that time (6:10). Had Nehemiah been stampeded into taking this lawless and pointless action he would certainly have been discredited, but his sense of vocation as Israel's governor, guide, and mentor, plus, no doubt, his sense of being under God's protection already while he labored at God's work, kept him from panicking and prompted a forthright refusal of Shemaiah's suggestion. "Should a man like me [in my position] run away? Or should one like me [carrying my responsibilities as leader and example] go into the temple to save his life? I will not go!" (6:11).

Here, as on other occasions, Nehemiah showed great courage—a quality that has been well defined not as an absence of fear, but as a resolute doing of what is known to be right however much we feel afraid, disturbed, or hurt. Glancing back to Nehemiah's admission that when Artaxerxes asked what his trouble was "I was very much afraid" (2:2), John White comments: "He probably experienced fear many times in his life, but at the start of the story he established the habit that became of real service to him later—moving ahead in spite of fear. It was in that moment that he enrolled in God's school of courage."[6] Through God he behaved throughout as a brave man. We saw his moral courage in his public confession of anti-social moneylending; now we see comparable physical courage in his response to Shemaiah.

Let us be clear that such courage is not, and never was, natural. Some unimaginative people are naturally insensitive to danger, but the bravery that takes risks for God, knowing how dangerous they are, is not natural: it is God's own gift and has a supernatural source. Christians locate this source in Spirit-taught understanding of the cross of Christ, of which the hymn rightly says:

> Inscribed upon the cross we see
>   In shining letters, "God is Love";
> He bears our sins upon the tree;
>   He brings us mercy from above.

> The cross! it takes our guilt away;
>   It holds the fainting spirit up;
> It cheers with hope the gloomy day,
>   And sweetens every bitter cup.

> It makes the coward spirit brave,
>   And nerves the feeble arm for fight;
> It takes death's terror from the grave
>   And gilds the bed of death with light.

In cultures where active Christians are seen as an eccentric minority, and are opposed from time to time in the name of prudence and common sense, the courage modeled by Nehemiah and many more biblical characters with him is a grace that must be sought constantly; for we cannot manage without it, and nature alone will not supply it.

Also, we should note that Nehemiah here showed great discernment. He saw through Shemaiah's deception at once and realized "that God had not sent him, but that he had prophesied against me because Tobiah and Sanballat had hired him. He had been hired to intimidate me so that I would commit a sin" (6:12-13). As art connoisseurs will identify an El Greco or a Van Gogh by its style, so Sherlock Holmes once identified a complex crime as "a Moriarty," meaning that it bore the marks of that master-criminal's mind. And in the same way, Nehemiah was able to identify Shemaiah's action as "a Tobiah and Sanballat"—precisely the sort of thing this pair would do. Discernment may be defined as the ability to see what you are looking at and to assess it by appropriate criteria. Spiritual discernment is a matter of perceiving the qualities, tendencies, and likely sources of proposals and policies that relate to God and his kingdom. Though such discernment may have a basis in natural shrewdness, it comes to fruition only through a sustained attunement to God and a habit of asking oneself at every point in life what makes for his glory (that is, his own self-expression and his creatures' appreciation and adoration of him). Asking this question appears as Nehemiah's constant habit of mind, and we may confidently say that his ability to see to the heart of issues and to sniff out the stratagems of his opponents was a God-taught spinoff from it. In our day spiritual confusions abound (and surely it was always so): for us, therefore, as for Nehemiah, and for all faithful souls since his time, spiritual discernment is a prime need, which nature alone will not supply, and which therefore must be sought from God through godliness as a way and style of life.

LEADERS AS TARGETS

In Satan's war on the saints and on the church, the war in which temptation is his method and destruction his immediate goal, it is a rather grim law that the higher one's exposure and the greater one's influence as a leader of others, the more one's personal standards and political wisdom will be put under attack. It is obvious that disgracing or distracting the leader is an excellent way of daunting, holding back, or otherwise sidelining the followers. Leaders have something of a Pied Piper quality: they are thought of as wise and far-seeing, and people trust their judgment and follow in their steps; so if they can be allured into bypaths and blind alleys, they will take many with them, and Satan will score heavily. Also, leaders live in something of a goldfish bowl, so that when leadership scandals break, the damage and discouragement will be large-scale and widespread. In the New Testament, Paul's letters to Timothy and Titus, which we call the Pastorals because their theme is the pastoral leader's role, concentrate not on skills to learn but on the qualities of zeal, goodness, steadiness, and wisdom that the leader must maintain and model. This is because Paul is so conscious of "the devil's trap" (1 Tim. 3:7; 2 Tim. 2:26) set for those who lead. Nehemiah's story, as we have seen, abundantly illustrates his point.

Spiritual warfare involves all Christians, and the classic passage (Eph. 6:10-18) in which Paul speaks in infantry-man's terms of the resources God gives for this conflict is addressed to believers as such. Clearly, though, it has a special relevance for leaders. How necessary it is for a leader to have "the belt of truth buckled round your waist"—the "truth" here being the revealed truth of God in the Scriptures generally and in the gospel of Christ particularly. How important it is that a leader should have "the breastplate of righteousness in place"—"righteousness" here signifying what Paul elsewhere calls "good works," that is, uprightness and integrity of life in covenant with God. How vital it is, too, that a leader should have "feet fitted with the readiness that comes from the gospel of peace"—"readiness" here meaning maneuverability, the capacity to run, jump, adjust, and quickly change one's position, or else stand firm, poised, balanced, and ready to counter-attack, according to what the enemy's action requires. How crucial it is that a leader should be carrying and using "the shield of faith, with which you can extinguish all the flaming arrows of the evil one"—these "arrows" being thoughts that embody doubt, despair, unbelief, misbelief, self-pity, irresponsibility, bitterness against God, and malice against people. How indispensable it is that a leader should have his head protected by "the helmet of salvation"—"salvation" here meaning conscious, assured enjoyment of loving fellowship with Jesus the Saviour—and his hand wielding "the sword of the Spirit, which is the word of God"—"sword" meaning here that with which you drive the enemy away, as Jesus drove Satan away in the desert by quoting from the Law of Moses on true godliness and committing himself to live by the words he cited (Mt. 4:1-11).

One of the all-time sitcom classics of international TV was *Dad's Army*, an affectionate take-off of the Home Guard, Britain's amateur defense force against invasion during the Second World War. One of the tag-lines of the series belonged to the oldest member of the troop, a dignified dodderer who at times of stress would shout, "Don't panic! Don't panic!" That is the word with which to end this chapter; it is the equivalent of the Bible's often-repeated "Do not be afraid," or "Fear not," as the *King James Version* regularly rendered it. Satan through his agents, devilish and human, assaults all Christians, and leaders, it seems, most fiercely; all Christians, therefore, and leaders supremely, must learn to pray with Nehemiah, "Now strengthen my hands" (6:9)—not only for constructive ministry, corresponding to the building of Jerusalem's wall, but also for mortal combat, corresponding to the sequence of defensive measures against Jerusalem's enemies (who said, "we . . . will kill them," 4:11; "they were scheming to harm me," 6:2). When this is truly the prayer of our hearts, then the outcome of the conflict is assured, for leaders no less than for others caught in the fight. Those who seek God's strength will find it. The outcome will be salvation, not destruction: Satan will be thwarted and the church built up, and the God through whose help all the work is done will be glorified.

CHAPTER SIX

Times of Refreshing

This chapter takes a bird's-eye view of everything recorded from the completion of Jerusalem's new wall (6:15) to its solemn dedication (12:27-43). Thus it covers a lot of ground, as much indeed in verse length as it has taken five chapters of exposition to cover up to this point. There are reasons, however, that make this sudden speed-up an appropriate move.

First, chapters 7–12 of Nehemiah's book have one sustained theme—namely, the restoring of the Jewish people in the holy city—*Israel Alive Again*, to quote the happy title of a recent commentary.[1] The theme is dealt with in four sections: establishing the community, 7:1-73a; learning the Law, 7:73b–8:18; renewing the covenant, 9:1–10:39; peopling the city, 11:1–12:26. But it is a single topic, and one that is more easily grasped through an overview than by burrowing into the mass of detail that the text itself presents.

Second, our focus of interest in the present exposition is Nehemiah himself, and from 7:5 to 12:26 he virtually drops out of the story. He receives just three mentions, each in the third person as "Nehemiah the governor" (8:9-10; 10:1; 12:26). Clearly he was not the first drafter of any of this material, although by incorporating it in his memoirs he makes it his own. Nothing, however, is lost for our understanding of Nehemiah by a briefer treatment of this part of his book than his own narrative has received thus far (and will receive again when it resumes in 12:27).

Third, these chapters bulge with lists of names, of which over 250 are of persons otherwise unknown. This is the sort of material, as was said earlier, that a modern writer would put in an appendix. That does not, of course, mean that these items were never of any importance. The family census of returned exiles in 7:6-73, which Nehemiah consulted as a check-list when, as he tells us, "my God put it into my heart to assemble the nobles, the officials and the common people for registration by families" (7:5), and the roster of returned priests and Levite sub-clans that is reproduced in 12:1-26 were vastly important at the time: they made it possible to identify who was authentically Jewish and so a proper person to be part of the Jerusalem community, and also (even more important) to see who was qualified for temple ministry, which God had restricted to the Levitical blood line. So, too, the list of priests, Levites, and other leaders who with Nehemiah affixed their names to the national covenant for faithfulness to God's Law (10:1-27) had an importance that can only be measured by the importance of the covenant itself. As for the honorific lists of Levites and other religious leaders who stood with Ezra (8:4, 7; 9:4-5), their importance for Nehemiah's first readers will be obvious to any of us who celebrate ancestors who fought at Waterloo or Gettysburg or have senior relatives who served with Montgomery in North Africa or Nimitz in the Pacific. Merely to note the existence of the lists is, however, sufficient for our present purposes, and that means that we can pass through these chapters more briskly than one might have expected.

GOD TAKES OVER

The theme of the book of Nehemiah as a whole, and perhaps we should say here the theme of Ezra—Nehemiah as a literary twosome, is the refounding of Israel as a nation-family and a nation-church after the desolation of the exile and the near-century of unsuccessful attempts to set Jerusalem on its feet that preceded Nehemiah's governorship. What Ezra—Nehemiah tells us is that it pleased God through the work of these two men, Ezra the teacher and Nehemiah the organizer, to set up his people once more as his worshiping church on earth in its prescribed Old Testament form. "By the end of these two books the former exiles have had their chief structures, visible and invisible, re-established, and their vocation confirmed, to be a people instructed in the law and separated from the nations."[2] The rebuilding of the walls appears as preparatory to the reordering of community life around the temple liturgy and the practice of holiness, that is, purity—moral, ritual, and racial—to the Lord, according to the specifics of his command.

Ezra, who has not appeared in Nehemiah's story thus far but is just about to, was a priest, a scholar, and a teacher of the Law (what was called a *scribe*, 8:1, 4, 9, 13). He was also a saintly person, a man of outstandingly deep and sensitive devotion, as we shall shortly see. Artaxerxes, following the benevolent multi-faith policy of all the Persian monarchs, had sent him to Jerusalem in 458 B.C. to teach the divine law and to make sure that worship in the temple, which had been rebuilt in 516 B.C., was being properly carried out (see Ezra 7). All we know of Ezra's ministry in the city to this point is that shortly after his arrival he led the people's leaders in a large-scale purging out of mixed marriages (Ezra 9–10). Since then, though he had clearly gained respect as a teacher, as we shall shortly see, it does not appear that his influence

had been very great. Now, however, he is about to come into
his own.

Yet that is not the way to put it. For in the great central
event of Israel's spiritual rehabilitation, in which Ezra's
major role was played, it was very clear from the outset that
God had taken over and was in charge, and if anyone was
coming into his own it was he himself, the Lord. Here is
the story.

> All the people assembled as one man in the square
> before the Water Gate. They told Ezra the scribe to
> bring out the Book of the Law of Moses, which the
> LORD had commanded for Israel.
>
> So on the first day of the seventh month Ezra the
> priest brought the Law before the assembly, which was
> made up of men and women and all who were able to
> understand. He read it aloud from daybreak till noon as
> he faced the square before the Water Gate in the pres-
> ence of the men, women and others who could under-
> stand. And all the people listened attentively to the Book
> of the Law.
>
> Ezra the scribe stood on a high wooden platform
> built for the occasion. Beside him on his right stood
> Mattithiah, Shema, Anaiah, Uriah, Hilkiah and
> Maaseiah; and on his left were Pedaiah, Mishael,
> Malkijah, Hashum, Hashbaddanah, Zechariah and
> Meshullam.
>
> Ezra opened the book. All the people could see him
> because he was standing above them; and as he opened
> it, the people all stood up. Ezra praised the LORD, the
> great God; and all the people lifted their hands and
> responded, "Amen! Amen!" Then they bowed down
> and worshiped the LORD with their faces to the ground.
>
> The Levites—Jeshua, Bani, Sherebiah, Jamin,
> Akkub, Shabbethai, Hodiah, Maaseiah, Kelita, Azariah,
> Jozabad, Hanan and Pelaiah—instructed the people in
> the Law while the people were standing there. They

read from the Book of the Law of God, making it clear
and giving the meaning so that the people could understand what was being read.

Then Nehemiah the governor, Ezra the priest and
scribe, and the Levites who were instructing the people
said to them all, "This day is sacred to the LORD your
God. Do not mourn or weep." For all the people had
been weeping as they listened to the words of the Law.

Nehemiah said, "Go and enjoy choice food and
sweet drinks, and send some to those who have nothing
prepared. This day is sacred to our Lord. Do not grieve,
for the joy of the LORD is your strength."

The Levites calmed all the people, saying, "Be still,
for this is a sacred day. Do not grieve."

Then all the people went away to eat and drink, to
send portions of food and to celebrate with great joy,
because they now understood the words that had been
made known to them.

On the second day of the month, the heads of all the
families, along with the priests and the Levites, gathered
around Ezra the scribe to give attention to the words of
the Law. They found written in the Law, which the
LORD had commanded through Moses, that the
Israelites were to live in booths during the feast of the
seventh month and that they should proclaim this word
and spread it throughout their towns and in Jerusalem:
"Go out into the hill country and bring back branches
from olive and wild olive trees, and from myrtles, palms
and shade trees, to make booths"—as it is written.

So the people went out and brought back branches
and built themselves booths on their own roofs, in their
courtyards, in the courts of the house of God and in the
square by the Water Gate and the one by the Gate of
Ephraim. The whole company that had returned from
exile built booths and lived in them. From the days of
Joshua son of Nun until that day, the Israelites had not
celebrated it like this. And their joy was very great.

Day after day, from the first day to the last, Ezra read
from the Book of the Law of God. They celebrated the
feast for seven days, and on the eighth day, in accor-
dance with the regulation, there was an assembly.

(Nehemiah 8)

When I say that God took over, I do not mean that he had
not been ruling over them all along. Nehemiah's statement
that the walls were rebuilt "with the help of our God" (6:16)
proclaims the contrary to that! What I mean, rather, is that
God now acted in a way that put his own human agents in
the shade. To use the biblical word, he *visited* his people, pre-
empting their attention and making his presence felt among
them in a way that had not been the case before. Moments
of this kind, when minds and hearts are inundated and overwhelmed by the reality of God in his holiness and grace,
belong to the history of most movements of spiritual
advance, and days and weeks together of this experience—
more, therefore, than just isolated moments—belong to the
history of those supreme visitations that we call revivals.
What occurred in Jerusalem in the seventh month of 444
B.C. was a revival in this sense, as we shall see. It will help our
understanding of it, however, if first we glance again at the
overall situation from Nehemiah's point of view.

A TASK UNFINISHED

A good man's work is never done, says the proverb, and that
is certainly how things are in the service of God. The more
you have done, the more you see still waiting to be done. As
pastors know, completing a major development in a
church's life, one that has required maximum motivation
and effort, probably with strain and pain into the bargain,
may be felt and rejoiced in as a milestone, but it soon comes
to present itself as no more than a stepping-stone to the next
task. A brief breathing-space is doubtless in order, but then

it must be down to work again. When you climb my favorite
Welsh mountain, the highest outside Snowdonia, by my
favorite route, there are two places where you are sure you
are seeing the top ahead of you; but when you get to the
point you saw, you find it was only a fold in the terrain, and
the real summit is still a distance away. That is a good illustration of how Christian ministry feels in all its forms. It is
a familiar experience that in family and business life goals
and targets are like Chinese boxes—each one you reach
proves to have another waiting inside it—and this is
supremely so in the church.

There is always more to be done, and the doing is not
meant to stop until this life is over. Even when the state of
our health limits our doing to praying, as in old age it com-
monly does, that remains true. No doubt much of this
passed through Nehemiah's mind on that momentous
September day when the last gate was set in place and the
wall was truly finished, for the work he had come to
Jerusalem to do was not finished; indeed, it had hardly
started and was going to require of him a great deal more
effort yet.

What was that work? It was to bring into being, with
God's help, a truly godly, adult, mature Jewish community
in "the holy city" (11:1, 18). Prior to the rebuilding of its
walls, Jerusalem had been an open city, broken-down, economically depressed, low in morale, under-populated (7:4),
and in no way glorious for God. Now that the walls were up,
the human factors in this sad situation had to be attended to.

Good community leadership at what we would call
middle-management level was obviously needed; so "I put
in charge of Jerusalem my brother Hanani, along with
Hananiah the commander of the citadel, because he was a
man of integrity and feared God more than most men do"
(7:2). Nehemiah was appointing to key posts strong men
whose priorities matched his own, whose public life would

set an inspiring example, and who would take some of the administrative load off his shoulders. (And how important it is in the local church that pastors recruit, if they do not inherit, a team of lay leaders with whom they see eye to eye, and whose influence and efficiency they can trust!)

Again, the sense that Jerusalem's inhabitants were a community separated from the world in order to be a beacon for God had to be nourished and strengthened, starting really from nowhere; so "I said to them, 'The gates of Jerusalem are not to be opened until the sun is hot'" (7:3). Till well on in the morning each day the world was to remain outside; this would help the people inside to develop their awareness of being different, and of being called to be different, just because they were the people of God. (And how important it is that Christian churches and families should take time and make the effort to develop this same awareness today!)

Finally, "the city was large and spacious, but there were few people in it" (7:4): the families of the returned exiles had scattered through the countryside to eke out a living as small land-holders, and a new population had to be recruited. (And how important it is that local churches should reach out in evangelism, so that Christ's wedding banquet may be filled with guests!)

There was indeed much to be done.

And the domestic opposition was still there, now coalescing round Tobiah. Nehemiah describes how that opposition had been through the seven-plus weeks of furious wall-building. "In those days the nobles of Judah were sending many letters to Tobiah, and replies from Tobiah kept coming to them. For many in Judah were under oath to him" (both he and his son had married into the aristocracy); ". . . they kept reporting to me his good deeds and then telling him what I said. And Tobiah sent letters to intimidate me" (6:17-19). Nehemiah's perceptiveness, prayerfulness,

prudence, and persistence had so far enabled him to sur-
mount the opposition both of the political heavyweights
abroad (Sanballat and Geshem) and of the "fifth column" at
home (the subversive nobles), and also of Tobiah, who was
in league with both. Now that Jerusalem was a fortified city,
with its gates closed each evening, perhaps as early as siesta
time, and guards on the walls (7:3), Sanballat and Geshem
were unlikely to cause any more trouble; but Tobiah was a
different matter. He was close to Jewish top people, who saw
him as a good fellow; who looked down their noses at
Nehemiah as a low-class Johnny-come-lately—"not one of
us"; who had never as a body been enthused about rebuilding the walls (see 3:5); and who had now become very angry
at Nehemiah's clamping down on their moneylending and
slave trade and humiliating them for it in public. So
Nehemiah could only expect that Tobiah would be pulling
and conspiring against him on a permanent basis, and he
needed to prepare for more conflict accordingly.

(And how important it is that pastors and pastoral leaders be equally realistic about continuing opposition in the
churches they serve! When change in established procedures is proposed, there will always be some who oppose it,
thinking it will be more comfortable if things go on just as
before. When proposed changes would reduce someone's
power and influence, there will always be opposition from
persons—not necessarily the holders of power themselves—
who think it will be more comfortable for power to remain
where it now is. When a move forward in ministry is suggested or introduced, there will always be some who stand
against it as both needless and uncomfortable. Comfort of
one sort or another in what Pierre Berton hauntingly called
"the comfortable pew,"[3] a comfort of which somnolence and
inertia form a large part, is the supreme desire of many in the
churches, and anything that threatens to disrupt their comfortable routine will be resented. As clinker keeps a coal fire

from giving out full heat, so Satan sees to it that the clinker factor regularly operates in Christian congregations—that is, that coolness, latent or overt, towards the leadership puts a damper on spiritual progress. It is surprising how often a congregation served by a lively minister has at its heart an unresponsive group of old stagers who were there before he came and whose chief concern now is to see him go. How necessary it is that leaders be prepared for this, and not expect anything else!)

Nehemiah, with all these things in his mind, would have been praying and planning for the next stages of the fight for a godly Jerusalem from the day the walls were finished. What actually happened five days later, however, on the first day of Tisri, was something he could not have anticipated, any more than (at present, anyway) we can predict earthquakes. *God broke in* and in one day did more towards the desired goal than Nehemiah could have asked or imagined.

A SPIRITUAL NEED

"When the seventh month [Tisri] came," we read, "and the Israelites had settled in their towns . . ." (i.e., gone home after weeks of camping in Jerusalem to finish the walls; cf. 4:22)— the phrase echoes the previous verse, a tag-trick that the Old Testament often uses to link things together—"all the people [came back in from the country and] assembled as one man in the square before the Water Gate. They told Ezra the scribe to bring out the Book of the Law of Moses" (7:73b-8:1).

What was this?

It was certainly a planned occasion, for a high wooden platform had been built in readiness for Ezra's reading (8:4-5). And it is natural to suppose that the planner was Nehemiah. It is easy to imagine him announcing the meeting as he sent each detachment of his work force home—"Now remember, be back here on the first of the month for the day when we will all learn the Law of our God together." The need for everyone to know God's revelation of his will and ways in the *Torah* (the five books of Moses) was very clear and obvious: because the Law was locked up in Hebrew while all the people spoke Aramaic, and because no nationwide attempt to teach the Law had been made since the exile at least, ordinary folk were deeply ignorant of its contents, and ignorance makes it impossible to serve and please God. A massive program of educating people in the divine law was very urgently needed.

The same was true in sixteenth-century England, when William Tyndale went abroad and hazarded his life (which eventually he forfeited) in order to translate the Scriptures, and Archbishop Thomas Cranmer anchored a copy of the Great Bible in every parish church, and King Edward VI appointed a half-dozen preachers to go up and down England full-time expounding the Bible and preaching the gospel, and the Puritans began creating the popular expository literature that did so much to make their England the land of the Book. Nehemiah, one supposes, was aware of the need for a learning program from the day he arrived and planned this educational venture around Ezra from the start, thus pushing the gentle scholar-preacher out in front to deploy his expertise as what we would call a Bible teacher. A good leader admits his own limitations, appreciates the gifts of others, and knows how to pass leadership to someone better qualified than himself to do a particular job; and that is what we see happening here. Nehemiah the layman put Ezra the scholar in charge of the large-scale teaching enterprise that he had in view.

It is worth observing, before we move on, that a counterpart of what Nehemiah saw to be needed in Jerusalem in the mid-fifth century B.C. is just as badly needed in the modern West. Parents no longer teach their children the Bible at home; preaching in the church is often topical and superfi-

cial rather than expository and theological, and Sunday
school teaching is often very rudimentary as far as the Bible
is concerned; and the public educational system, the media,
and the press, both popular and academic, all treat
Christianity as a dead letter, only surviving as a hobby for
persons of an unusual type. So there is not the least encouragement in our culture to become biblically literate, and the
net result is a generation frighteningly and pathetically ignorant of the Word of God. No significant movement towards
God can be expected while this remains so.

A SPIRITUAL DESIRE

It is one thing to announce a meeting; it is quite another
thing for people to come to it. Nehemiah must have won-
dered what sort of a crowd his meeting would draw, indeed
whether it would draw a crowd at all. There was no guarantee that after their few days at home the builders would be
back in the city en masse for the study day, still less that they
would bring their families and friends; nor was there any
guarantee that the minority whose homes were in Jerusalem
would come. But that is what happened. Very early in the
morning "*all* the people assembled *as one man* in the square
before the Water Gate"—men, women, and "others who
were able to understand" (8:1-3)—that is, older children.
There was shared expectation, excitement, and impatience;
the great crowd was eager to get going; the desire to learn
God's Law was conscious, pervasive, and strong; the sense
that this was going to be a wonderful day ran through the
whole gathering. People called out for the proceedings to
start; "*they told* Ezra the scribe to bring out the Book of the
Law of Moses." Imagine an impatient audience at a rock
concert picking up the chant, "We—want—Ezra," saying it
over and over, louder and louder, and you get some idea of
the feelings being expressed. Yet in their eagerness the peo-

ple were serious; they were not there for entertainment—
they meant business. They knew that this was a time when
God was doing great things for Israel, and they did not want
to miss any of what North Americans would call "the good-
ies." In a real though unfocused way, they looked forward to
hearing from God.

What had happened? In a word, this: the Holy Spirit had
worked on these people, giving them an interest in God, a
concern for divine things, and a desire for God's blessing that
was altogether out of the ordinary. True as is Augustine's
famous statement that our hearts are restless till they find rest
in God, fallen human beings do not naturally turn Godward
in their restlessness, but look to other things for contentment
instead. It takes the Spirit of God to generate active desire for
God and a purposeful seeking of him. In God's sovereign
strategy for world history there are times when the Spirit
works with particular power to stir up this motivation, not just
in some few individuals but in entire communities, and this
was one such time.

Another era of the same kind was the mid-eighteenth
century, when the English-speaking world on both sides of
the Atlantic experienced much of the Spirit's action in awakening spiritual concern at this initial level. Most amazing in
the story of the great international revival that was sparked
and sustained by the preaching of George Whitefield,
Howell Harris, Daniel Rowland, the Wesley brothers, John
Berridge, William Grimshaw, Jonathan Edwards, the
Tennents, Samuel Davies, and many lesser lights was the size
of the crowds that gathered when visits from leading preachers were announced. Whitefield, with his huge, beautiful
voice, dramatic style, and unique power of personal address,
drew the largest numbers—between ten and twenty thousand was usual when he preached out-of-doors; but all of
them spoke to gatherings of thousands on occasion. We may
ask, what is the source of this consuming concern to be

preached to, which contrasts so strikingly with what most of us feel and see today? Hope of being entertained, relief of boredom, or idle interest in what interests others are not sufficient answers, though doubtless some of the listeners stopped short at this level. But the only adequate explanation is that the Holy Spirit of God was working in power to stir up a sense of spiritual compulsion—compulsion, that is, to be as it were within hailing distance of God, should he have something relevant to say. And that is clearly how it was in Jerusalem on "the first day of the seventh month" of 444 B.C.

A SPIRITUAL EXERCISE

"Ezra . . . brought the Law. . . . He read it aloud from daybreak till noon . . ." (five or six hours!). "And all the people listened attentively to the Book of the Law" (8:2-3). That is the summary statement of what occurred; the detailed narrative follows, in 8:4-12. There we read that Ezra, who was worship leader as well as captain of the teaching team, presided from his pulpit-platform (the Hebrew word means "tower"), flanked by a platform party of thirteen. As he opened the Book of the Law, "the people all stood up," in an apparently spontaneous gesture of reverence. Worship began the day: "Ezra praised the LORD, the great God; and all the people lifted their hands and responded, 'Amen! Amen!' Then they bowed down and worshiped the LORD with their faces to the ground."

After that, a posse of thirteen trained Levites, stationed presumably at different points in the crowd, "instructed the people in the Law while the people were standing there." (These, of course, were days before public address equipment was invented.) "They read from the Book of the Law of God, making it clear and giving the meaning so that the people could understand what was being read" (8:8). The task was apparently twofold. First, the Levites had to translate from Hebrew into Aramaic, the dialect developed out of Hebrew that had become the spoken language of Palestine. This was comparable to the task of putting Chaucer's poetry into modern English. Then they had to spell out the application, so that their listeners would see what law-keeping to the Lord would mean for them in practice. The natural supposition is that Ezra would read a section and then pause while the Levites translated and explained; then he would read a further section, and so on. All this had evidently been planned out and rehearsed in advance, and it worked well. The Levites labored to teach, the crowd labored to learn, and, as 8:12 says, everybody "understood."

So more than five hours passed, with the people standing throughout, and with no coffee break or anything like it. The question, were they serious about what they were doing? seems to answer itself. They were there because they actually wanted to learn the Law, and they were exerting themselves in doing just that.

All forms of exercise, whether physical or mental, require exertion, and effort in worthwhile activities should never be grudged. Writes Paul to Timothy: "Train yourself to be godly. For physical training is of some value, but godliness has value for all things" (1 Tim. 4:7-8). A basic dimension of self-training in godliness is learning from the Bible to live by God's truth, and those who do not expend effort in exercising themselves at this point sentence themselves to come short of real godliness at many points. The Jews at the Water Gate were profoundly right to take time out for serious exertion at the first possible moment in grasping the revealed will of God.

How different, then, was the attitude of these Israelites from that which is common—all too common—among modern Western Christians! It is ironic to reflect that in a day when the Bible is the world's most widely circulated book, and Bible study is commended by Roman Catholics as well as

Protestants, and English-speaking Christians have more good translations, study Bibles, and other helps to understanding than any previous generation anywhere in the world, learning the contents of the Bible is a more neglected discipline, and knowledge of those contents is a rarer thing to find, than at any time since the Reformation. The trouble is threefold.

First, biblical criticism tells us that the specifics of the Bible cannot be trusted and therefore are not worth learning, so we pass them by. Second, liberal theology tells us that Christianity is essentially an ethical ethos, and the Bible's own emphasis on God-taught doctrine, given to be learned, was never anything but a mistake. (Does this mean that apostolic writers like Paul and John misunderstood the Christianity they taught and had hold of the wrong end of the stick from the start? In an important sense, yes. Liberal theology requires that conclusion.)

And third, our culture tells us that apart from technical professional stuff, only a smattering of knowledge about anything is needed to see us through, so that it would be rather naive for a Christian to spend much time learning details of any sort about Christianity. But the truth is that as the desire to learn what God has revealed in Scripture, so that we may serve him by response to his Word, is Spirit-given and enlivening, so a lack of willingness so to do is Spirit-quenching and deadening. So if we wonder why modern Western churches so conspicuously lack spiritual maturity and are so far from seeing spiritual revival and impacting secular society in a significant way, here is part at least of the answer.

A SPIRITUAL EXPERIENCE

At noon, so we read, Nehemiah, Ezra, and the Levites "said to them all, 'This day is sacred to the LORD your God. Do not mourn or weep.' For all the people had been weeping as they listened to the words of the Law" (8:9).

Weeping! Why? Because of the impact that understanding of God's Word was making on their hearts. People weep when they are overcome with emotion, and the emotions that cause tears are occasioned by vivid realizations of particular realities. The root of spiritual revival both in individuals and in communities (individuals, that is, in the mass) was, is, and always will be vivid realizations of God's holiness, goodness, and mercy, and of the perversity, shamefulness, offensiveness, and suicidal folly that he sees in our personal sins. Mourning and grief for sin will thence naturally result; and when these realizations of the truth about God and ourselves are clear and strong, the tears may very well flow.

Weeping under the ministry of the Word has never been a common thing, because this intensity of realization does not often come about. The reasons for that have to do partly with God and partly with people, and among people partly with preachers and partly with hearers. The Holy Spirit, who alone induces such realization in otherwise hard hearts, is too rarely invoked in a serious way by either preachers or congregations, and is too often obstructed and quenched by self-absorbed casualness about serving God, deep-level unconcern as to whether or not we please him, and deep-rooted unwillingness to face up to moral and behavioral challenges in our lives. Yet there are times when the Spirit empowers applicatory preaching to induce devastatingly vivid realizations of God's greatness, goodness, and closeness, and of the sinfulness of our sin. Here, for instance, is an account given by one Puritan to another of a midweek service at which he was present, early in the seventeenth century.

> Mr. Rogers was . . . on the subject of . . . the Scriptures. And . . . he falls into an expostulation with the people

about their neglect of the Bible . . . he personates God
to the people, telling them, 'Well, I have trusted you so
long with my Bible; you have slighted it, it lies in such
and such houses all covered with dust and cobwebs; you
care not to listen to it. Do you use my Bible so? Well,
you shall have my Bible no longer.' And he takes up the
Bible from his cushion, and seemed as if he were going
away with it and carrying it from them; but immediately
turns again and personates the people to God, falls down
on his knees, cries and pleads most earnestly, 'Lord,
whatever thou dost to us, take not thy Bible from us; kill
our children, burn our houses, destroy our goods; only
spare us thy Bible, only take not away thy Bible.' And
then he personates God again to the people: 'Say you so?
Well, I will try you a while longer; and here is my Bible
for you. I will see how you will use it, whether you will
love it more . . . observe it more . . . practice it more, and
live more according to it.' By these actions . . . he put all
the congregation into so strange a posture that . . . the
place was a mere Bochim, the people generally . . .
deluged with their own tears; and . . . he himself, when
he got out was fain to hang a quarter of an hour upon
the neck of his horse weeping before he had power to
mount; so strange an impression was there upon him,
and generally upon the people, upon having been
expostulated with for the neglect of the Bible.[4]

The teaching given to the Water Gate congregation did
not involve pulpit dramatics of this kind; yet it confronted
them with truths about God and themselves that they had
not faced up to before, and at a time when they had deliberately opened themselves to God to an unusual degree. The
Holy Spirit had stirred them to seriousness in laying hold of
their identity as God's people and seeking his way for their
lives, and had given them a humble willingness to be taught
it from God's own Word. It is natural to suppose that the
vivid realization of the holiness, goodness, and closeness of

"the LORD, the great God" had begun to dawn within them through the quality of Ezra's initial praying, before the teaching began. Ezra's own sense of the awesomeness of God, ever present and at work in great goodness and great severity ("The gracious hand of our God is on everyone who looks to him, but his great anger is against all who forsake him," Ezra 8:22), was exceedingly strong. We read that when Ezra first discovered how widespread and well established was the sin of Jews marrying pagans he ripped his clothes, tore out some of his hair, knelt before the temple, and voiced on Israel's behalf one of the most poignant confessions of sin against the God of grace that can be found in the Bible or anywhere else.

And then we read that "while Ezra was praying and confessing, weeping and throwing himself down before the house of God, a large crowd of Israelites . . . gathered round him. They too wept bitterly . . ." (Ezra 10:1). Enlarging people's realization of God's reality, and so deepening their perceptions of grace and sin, is a major part of some people's ministry; it was so, for instance, with the late Martyn Lloyd-Jones, as any who heard him will testify, and it looks as if the same was true of Ezra. But be that as it may, the certain fact is that by midday the Water Gate assembly was so overwhelmed by what it had learned of the work and will of God, the holy Creator, who had chosen and saved and separated Israel to be his holy people, that it was in tears, and the teaching had to be broken off.

"Nehemiah said, 'Go and enjoy choice food and sweet drinks, and send some to those who have nothing prepared. This day is sacred to our Lord. Do not grieve, for the joy of the LORD is your strength'" (8:10). He, Ezra, and the Levites saw that the people were weeping out of grief and gladness together: grief that they had gone on so long without getting clear on what pleased and displeased their God, so that in fact they had failed to serve him properly, and gladness that instead of casting them off for this he had mercifully sent agents to restore their city and to teach them his Word, so that they might know how to love and serve him for the future. While the grief looked back, the gladness looked ahead, and the leaders wisely judged that publicly expressing the gladness rather than the grief was the appropriate thing to do. Weeping in grief after several hours of standing and concentrating would in any case exhaust the people's spirits, and should they feel, as well they might if grief took over, that they should fast to express what they felt, their bodies would soon be exhausted too.

The course of action that the leaders pressed on them was better from every point of view. "The joy of the LORD is your strength," said Nehemiah (one imagines him shouting it from the platform); so rejoice!—feast in joyful generosity, rather than fast in sad self-absorption! "Go and enjoy . . . Do not grieve." Thus he brought the meeting to an end.

"Can you conceive modern organizers of a revival meeting behaving in such a manner?" asks John White. "We feel we have it made when people begin to weep!"[5] And then, he might have added, we prolong the meeting, thinking we gain great spiritual mileage from their tears. But Ezra and Nehemiah knew what modern revivalists sometimes seem not to know—namely, that there is nothing intrinsically magical or necessarily spiritual about tears (people cry, some very easily, at all sorts of things); nor is there anything naturally beneficial in churning people up, or keeping them churned up, by calculated emotional manipulation and appeal. What mattered in Jerusalem in 444 B.C. was that the people's enlarged, deepened, and intensified realization of God's greatness, holiness, and goodness should be conserved and reinforced, and for that impromptu banquets, picnics perhaps, from which massive distribution to the poor would be made out of the sheer joy of knowing God, would do as well as anything.

The same principle applies today. Grief for sin, and joy in God's forgiveness and the assurance of his love, are not far from each other, for the God who convicts of sin is the God of mercy who saves, and repenting of sin and trusting Christ for forgiveness are two sides of the same coin. This two-sided, double-aspect turning to God is the basic discipline of each day's Christian living, and it is in relation to one or the other facet of it that the most vivid realizings of God, and enlargings of our grip on him, are likely to be given to us. And while there needs to be a time for grief as well as a time for joy, expressing our joy from the Lord can reinforce our spiritual realizations every bit as effectively as expressions of grief can do. Not all service of God need be somber.

A SPIRITUAL RESPONSE

The reality of the revival was further demonstrated the next day. God had given his people an appetite for his Word, a desire for the life of obedience, and an anxiety of conscience lest any of God's requirements be overlooked, and none of this had worn off. The women and children were not asked to appear again (probably it was assumed, with reason, that the previous day would have left them exhausted), but "the heads of all the families, along with the priests and the Levites, gathered round Ezra the scribe to give attention to the words of the Law" (8:13). They found that God required Israel to keep the Feast of Booths from the fifteenth to the twenty-second of that month, both as a harvest festival and as a memorial of the trek to the Promised Land, and they resolved to do it. The effort and, no doubt, inconvenience of collecting tree branches from all over, erecting shanties in Jerusalem wherever there was space to do so, and living in them for the festival week was taken in stride; the joy of obedience and of knowing that this pleased God carried all before it. "Their joy was very great" (8:17).

This was spiritual reality! This was life worth living! Nothing compares with knowing that you are doing God's will! Thus they felt, and they acted accordingly. "The scattered regulations for the festival," writes Derek Kidner, "were all searched out and followed with a will. Verse 15 has taken up the instruction given in Leviticus 23:40 ff. to gather leafy branches; the last sentence of verse 17 chimes in with the note of *rejoicing* called for in Deuteronomy 16:13-15; and now [verse 18] we learn of the reading of *the law* prescribed in Deuteronomy 31:10-13 for every seventh year, and of the *solemn assembly* of Numbers 29:35."[6] Under Ezra's and Nehemiah's combined leadership, Israel was off and running in her new identity as the restored people of God.

Here, again, is a pattern of spiritual life that is as authentic today as it was two and a half millennia ago. When an adolescent or an adult finds new life in Jesus Christ, and when a drooping Christian undergoes any form of quickening or renewal, obeying God ceases to be a drudgery and becomes a delight, and pleasing God by doing what he asks becomes the chief joy of life. The continuing passion to please God was the sign of the genuineness of the Jerusalem revival, and a comparable passion is required as an indication of genuineness in all circles where spiritual life—that is, regenerate life, life made new by the Holy Spirit—is claimed to exist today.

A SPIRITUAL COMMITMENT

Out of the revival that began at the Water Gate on the first day of Tisri the most significant gesture of response to God's grace and visitation was still to come. On the twenty-fourth of that month, three and a half weeks later, a national day of repentance and recommitment was held.

. . . the Israelites gathered together, fasting and wearing sackcloth and having dust on their heads. Those of Israelite descent had separated themselves from all foreigners. They stood in their places and confessed their sins and the wickedness of their fathers. They stood where they were and read from the Book of the Law of the LORD their God for a quarter of the day [three hours], and spent another quarter in confession and in worshiping the LORD their God. (9:1-3)

9:5-38 gives the text of the solemn prayer that formed the centerpiece for the occasion. Maybe Ezra composed it; certainly its sentiments and style are fully in line with what we know of his mind. It blends together praise of God as Creator and as "a forgiving God, gracious and compassionate, slow to anger and abounding in love" (9:17); thanksgiving for his grace in Israel's history; confession of sin against him (disobedience, rebellion, blasphemy, arrogance, disregard, evil); justifying God as faithful throughout to "his covenant of love" (9:32) ("In all that has happened to us, you have been just; you have acted faithfully, while we did wrong," 9:33); a frank complaint that "we are in great distress" (9:36-37); and a firm commitment ("we are making a binding agreement, putting it in writing," 9:38). Made "with a curse and an oath," the commitment was "to follow the Law of God given through Moses the servant of God and to obey carefully all the commands, regulations and decrees of the LORD our God" (10:29).

Within this frame were then set five specific undertakings: first, to prohibit mixed marriages for both men and women; second, to preserve the holiness of Sabbaths by not making purchases from non-Israelites during them; third, to protect the poor, both by letting land lie fallow every seventh year (when the poor could help themselves to anything growing on it, according to Exodus 23:11) and also by forgiving all debts every seventh year, according to Deuteronomy 15:1-11; fourth, to present all the firstborn, both of one's family and of one's animals, at the temple, which would mean paying a price for the former and surrendering the latter (see Num. 18:14-19); and fifth, to provide money (temple tax), wood, and tithes to support the temple services: "We will not neglect the house of our God" (10:39; see vv. 30-39).

Over and above the intrinsic importance of these undertakings for a godly national life, they were clearly meant as tokens, guaranteeing that all the Law would be faithfully kept and demonstrating a resolve to put God first in everything. In themselves, however, they constituted an impressive expression of faith, hope, and love. For the members of an economically depressed community to forgo marrying foreign money and trading seven days a week, and to promise to pay redemption money for the firstborn (see Num. 18:14-16), to work a social system that had the rich in effect giving substantially to the poor every seven years, and to tithe everything regularly for the temple was audacious, costly, and self-denying. But what it expressed in positive terms was a resolve to obey God at all costs, with no half measures, and to trust him totally to bestow *shalom*—peace, well-being, harmony, prosperity— on his faithful, loyal people. Love to God and to neighbor, whereby one devoted oneself to the worship of the one and the welfare of the other, was to be every Israelite's way of life, and God, "who keeps his covenant of love," would bless them according to his promise.

Israel's overall commitment was thus something very much to admire. It was an expression of radical repentance, which meant a change of mind, heart, and life; a gesture of full consecration, which meant being separated from other peoples to be the people of God; and a gateway into the life of faith, in which God would be relied on for everything.

It models the commitment that should mark the Christian church today—Christians marrying Christians and setting up Christian homes; Christians viewing their time, life, health, wealth, abilities, and influence as gifts from God of which they are stewards and on which God himself always has first claim; Christians being generous in the face of human need and responsible in giving (tithing? at least!—and when one can, doing more) to maintain the church's ministries and personnel.

The final expression of Israel's commitment was the willingness of the leaders to relocate their homes in Jerusalem, and the willingness of all the people to be selected by lot to do the same. Ten percent were chosen in this way to live in the city—not for their own sake, but for Jerusalem's sake, to make it a strong community that truly honored God and displayed his glory. "The people commended all the men who volunteered to live in Jerusalem" (11:2), and they were right to do so. When we choose places to live, is our first thought to please ourselves, or to be useful to God?

A SPIRITUAL CELEBRATION

12:27-43 tells of the ceremonial procession and praises with which the rebuilt wall was dedicated to God. It was a day of uninhibited delight, with thanksgiving as its keynote. "On that day they offered great sacrifices, rejoicing because God had given them great joy. The women and children also rejoiced. The sound of rejoicing in Jerusalem could be heard far away" (12:43). Do we praise God like this when he blesses us? Exuberance, carnival-style, can easily become carnal and unspiritual, but surely the exalted intensity of this day of worship, an exalted intensity that finds expression in many of the Psalms, has something to say to us today.

Two choirs, specially gathered for the occasion and trained by choirmaster Jezrahiah (12:28, 31, 42), walked the walls singing and met in the temple for more songs of praise and thanks, backed now by cymbals, harps, lyres, and trumpets (12:27, 41). Singing was the order of the day. So it is constantly in the worship prescribed in both Testaments.

> This is not true of other religions. Many use repetitive chants. In some, clergy sing. But generally the religions of the world are grim things. . . . Christians write hymns . . . choruses . . . oratorios. Why is this? Obviously because Christianity is itself joyous. It is a response to the great acts of God on our behalf, particularly in the life, death, and resurrection of Jesus Christ, which secured our salvation.[7]

"Let the word of Christ dwell in you richly . . . as you sing psalms, hymns and spiritual songs with gratitude in your hearts to God," writes Paul (Col. 3:16). Do we sing enough? Enough to sustain our own joy in salvation? Enough to give God the honor and appreciation that is his due? How much singing to God have we done today—did we do yesterday—shall we plan to do tomorrow?

A SPIRITUAL PATHWAY

We do not know which Psalms they sang, but it is natural to guess that Psalms 78, 105, and 106, telling of God's blessing in past days, plus the Psalms of Ascent (120—134), written for pilgrims going up to Jerusalem to worship, were used; plus also Psalm 48, the last stanza of which in effect describes what they were doing:

> *Walk about Zion, go round her,*
> *count her towers,*

consider well her ramparts,
view her citadels,
that you may tell of them to the next generation.
(vv. 12-13)

Also, Psalm 135 would have suited the occasion
admirably, just as it makes a fitting part of the conclusion of
this chapter. Nehemiah 8–12 showed us something of God's
work of revival, and the extraordinary passion and power of
people's devotion when revival has touched their lives.
Repentance, which humbles, and praise, which excites, are
still the two activities which, with God's blessing, lead most
directly into spiritual renewing, and joy and self-giving are
still the two activities in which spiritual renewing most naturally expresses itself. We see it all here, and the story should
stir us to seek a similar quickening for ourselves. Responsive
meditation on Psalm 135, as we reflect on the way God visited and renewed his people in Nehemiah's day, might take
us some distance along the revival road.

Praise the LORD.
Praise the name of the LORD,
  praise him, you servants of the LORD,
  you who minister in the house of the LORD,
  in the courts of the house of our God.

Praise the LORD ,for the LORD is good;
  sing praise to his name, for that is pleasant.
For the LORD has chosen Jacob to be his own,
  Israel to be his treasured possession.

I know that the LORD is great,
  that our Lord is greater than all gods.
The LORD does whatever pleases him,
  in the heavens and on the earth,
  in the seas and all their depths.

> *He makes clouds rise from the ends of the earth;*
> *he sends lightning with the rain*
> *and brings out the wind from his storehouses. . . .*
>
> *The idols of the nations are silver and gold,*
> *made by the hands of men.*
> *They have mouths, but cannot speak,*
> *eyes, but they cannot see;*
> *they have ears, but cannot hear,*
> *nor is there breath in their mouths.*
> *Those who make them will be like them,*
> *and so will all who trust in them.*
>
> *O house of Israel, praise the LORD,*
> *O house of Aaron, praise the LORD,*
> *O house of Levi, praise the LORD,*
> *you who fear him, praise the LORD,*
> *Praise be to the LORD from Zion,*
> *to him who dwells in Jerusalem.*
>
> *Praise the LORD.*
>
> (vv. 1-7, 15-21)

And then we would do well to make the first half of Psalm 85 our own:

> *You showed favor to your land, O LORD;*
> *you restored the fortunes of Jacob.*
> *You forgave the iniquity of your people*
> *and covered all their sins.*
> *You set aside all your wrath*
> *and turned from your fierce anger.*
>
> *Restore us again, O God our Savior,*
> *and put away your displeasure toward us.*
> *Will you be angry with us forever?*
> *Will you prolong your anger through all generations?*

Will you not revive us again,
    that your people may rejoice in you?
Show us your unfailing love, O LORD,
    and grant us your salvation.

(vv. 1-7)

And if God enables us to go thus far—who can tell what
may happen next?

CHAPTER SEVEN

Back to Square One

C hildren's fairy stories tell us that good souls who survive specific evil attacks live happily ever after. Paperback romances, which like westerns, mysteries, and science fiction are really adult fairy stories, build on what P. G. Wodehouse described as the oldest plot in the world—boy meets girl, boy loses girl, boy gets girl—and then invite us to suppose that after finally falling into each other's arms the couple continue in permanent euphoria and tranquillity. But real life—the life of real relationships, real marriages, real jobs, real business operations, and so on—does not match these formulae, and the church's life least of all. It is a matter of divine promise that in heaven all our troubles will be over, but to expect any such state of affairs on earth, either in our personal lives or in the life of our churches, is fantasy and delusion. To indulge the delusion, as Satan, liar that he is, urges us to do, is to set ourselves up for wounding disappointments. It is vital that all Christians learn realism about this.

Within the church, the complaint that things never change is often heard, but in reality a conjunction of three distinct forces ensures the opposite—namely, that things will never simply stay put, or go on endlessly right after they have for the moment come right. The first force is human restlessness, which takes many forms, including sometimes, paradoxically enough, an energetic campaign of resisting change—but in such a way that the energy put into the project reveals deep restlessness of heart. (Tobiah's wheeling and dealing looks like an instance of this.) The second force is God's energy, working to transform people into a truer Christlikeness and a maturer holiness of life. The third force is Satan's energy, directed, as we saw, to corrupting the good things God has made and the good work that he is doing.

With these three forces pushing and pulling at the same time, you cannot wonder that within the frame of what looks like steadiness churches do not stay steady at all. There are ups and downs, wobbles, recoveries, and then more wobbles; lost vision and vitality may reappear, sometimes quite suddenly; and then after such moments of revival a negative reaction—you could call it the post-renewal blues—easily sets in.

No doubt this reaction need not happen and should not happen, but Scripture and experience alike show us that it often does. Where God has sent reformation, Satan will work, behind the scenes if not overtly, for deformation of all that was made new. Where God has enlivened the moribund, Satan will try to make the revival run out into either tyrannical legalism or zany antinomianism or proud fanaticism or equally proud skepticism; thus, one way or another he will labor to ensure that the revival produces as little long-term change for the better as possible. Satan's constant attacks on the church, and God's refusal to give up on it, thus guarantee recurring disappointments alongside periodic encouragements for those on whom the care of God's people falls. Which brings us to the seemingly anti-climactic narrative of Nehemiah 13.

> Eliashib the priest had been put in charge of the storerooms of the house of our God. He was closely associated with Tobiah, and he had provided him with a large

room formerly used to store the grain offerings and
incense and temple articles, and also the tithes of grain,
new wine and oil prescribed for the Levites, singers and
gatekeepers, as well as the contributions for the priests.

But while all this was going on, I was not in
Jerusalem, for in the thirty-second year of Artaxerxes
king of Babylon I had returned to the king. Some time
later I asked his permission and came back to Jerusalem.
Here I learned about the evil thing Eliashib had done in
providing Tobiah a room in the courts of the house of
God. I was greatly displeased and threw all Tobiah's
household goods out of the room. I gave orders to
purify the rooms, and then I put back into them the
equipment of the house of God, with the grain offerings
and the incense.

I also learned that the portions assigned to the Levites
had not been given to them, and that all the Levites and
singers responsible for the service had gone back to their
own fields. So I rebuked the officials and asked them,
"Why is the house of God neglected?" Then I called
them together and stationed them at their posts.

All Judah brought the tithes of grain, new wine and
oil into the storerooms. I put Shelemiah the priest,
Zadok the scribe, and a Levite named Pedaiah in charge
of the storerooms and made Hanan son of Zaccur, the
son of Mattaniah, their assistant, because these men
were considered trustworthy. They were made responsible for distributing the supplies to their brothers.

Remember me for this, O my God, and do not blot
out what I have so faithfully done for the house of my
God and its services.

In those days I saw men in Judah treading wine-
presses on the Sabbath and bringing in grain and load-
ing it on donkeys, together with wine, grapes, figs and
all other kinds of loads. And they were bringing all this
into Jerusalem on the Sabbath. Therefore I warned
them against selling food on that day. Men from Tyre

who lived in Jerusalem were bringing in fish and all kinds of merchandise and selling them in Jerusalem on the Sabbath to the people of Judah. I rebuked the nobles of Judah and said to them, "What is this wicked thing you are doing—desecrating the Sabbath day? Didn't your forefathers do the same things, so that our God brought all this calamity upon us and upon this city? Now you are stirring up more wrath against Israel by desecrating the Sabbath."

When evening shadows fell on the gates of Jerusalem before the Sabbath, I ordered the doors to be shut and not opened until the Sabbath was over. I stationed some of my own men at the gates so that no load could be brought in on the Sabbath day. Once or twice the merchants and sellers of all kinds of goods spent the night outside Jerusalem. But I warned them and said, "Why do you spend the night by the wall? If you do this again, I will lay hands on you." From that time on they no longer came on the Sabbath. Then I commanded the Levites to purify themselves and go and guard the gates in order to keep the Sabbath day holy.

Remember me for this also, O my God, and show mercy to me according to your great love.

Moreover, in those days I saw men of Judah who had married women from Ashdod, Ammon and Moab. Half of their children spoke the language of Ashdod or the language of one of the other peoples, and did not know how to speak the language of Judah. I rebuked them and called curses down on them. I beat some of the men and pulled out their hair. I made them take an oath in God's name and said: "You are not to give your daughters in marriage to their sons, nor are you to take their daughters in marriage for your sons or for yourselves. Was it not because of marriages like these that Solomon king of Israel sinned? Among the many nations there was no king like him. He was loved by his God, and God made him king over all Israel, but even he was led into sin by foreign women. Must we hear now that you too are doing all this terrible wickedness and are being unfaithful to our God by marrying foreign women?"

One of the sons of Joiada son of Eliashib the high priest was son-in-law to Sanballat the Horonite. And I drove him away from me.

Remember them, O my God, because they defiled the priestly office and the covenant of the priesthood and of the Levites.

So I purified the priests and the Levites of everything foreign, and assigned them duties, each to his own task. I also made provision for contributions of wood at designated times, and for the firstfruits.

Remember me with favor, O my God.

(Nehemiah 13:4-31)

This closing section of Nehemiah's book illustrates three general truths about the Christian church that need to be well understood.

COOLING DOWN

First: *mountaintop moments cannot be maintained in the church*.

My imagery here comes from the story of the Transfiguration, which tells how Jesus took Peter, James, and John up "a high mountain" (Mt. 17:1) in order to give them the overwhelming experience of seeing him momentarily glorified and talking with Moses and Elijah. Mountaintop experiences of God, precious though sometimes disorienting, in which God seals aspects of his truth and love on our hearts, are frequently given at revival times, to be remembered thereafter with awe and gratitude. No doubt there were many such experiences in late September and October, 444 B.C., during the momentous days of the Jerusalem visitation, when so much truth about God was becoming so clear to so many. But John White rightly flags the fact that preachers today sometimes try to manufacture mountaintop moments by playing on people's emotions:

> Many preachers use psychological manipulation without altogether realizing they are doing so. It is gratifying to perceive a powerful emotion gripping a congregation. We too easily jump to the conclusion that God is at work when in fact this may not be the case at all. This is why so much sterility follows powerful meetings: the power is sometimes psychological and not spiritual. Psychological manipulation cannot produce ongoing spiritual renewal.[1]

That is true; and it is also true that God does not in any case permit his people to live on the mountaintop. The disciples had to leave the mount of transfiguration and return with Jesus to the ordinary world at ground level; and after a genuine spiritual "high" has come our way so must we. Divine sovereignty operates here in an obvious fashion: as wise parents do not give their children endless candies, since too many candies would not be good for them, so God does not bestow mountaintop moments on a constant basis. For the Christian life to be all thrills would work against maturity and inner toughness, and ripening and toughening us is central to God's plan. Meanwhile, however, Christians are constantly tempted to let themselves cool off and grow slack in various ways. Thus it comes about that in actual experience God-given times of great spiritual intensity and major achievement in ministry are often followed by times of decline.

It was so in the New Testament period as a whole. On the Day of Pentecost in A.D. 30 the Holy Spirit was poured out in revival blessing, the disciples gained insights and lost their inhibitions, the truth about Jesus was clearly proclaimed and understood, 3,000 came to faith, and the church was up and running. The next two decades were a time of triumph, in which the gospel was racing ahead; it spread out from Jerusalem to Samaria and then into the Gentile world, and it is clear from the New Testament that in place after place there was spectacular initial success. But the New Testament ends with a letter addressed to each of seven churches by Jesus himself, with a long visionary appendix attached, and from this Book of Revelation, written probably in the nineties of the first century, it is clear that revival conditions had become a thing of the past. Sin and unfaithfulness, false doctrine and immoral conduct, complacency and hard-heartedness are all denounced, because they have all crept in; each church is laboring, and needing encouragement desperately. It is apparent that the "high" of the early days had now been followed by a "low," a flat period in which churches were flagging. And it is not only in Revelation that we are confronted with this spiritual decline; the pastoral epistles of Paul, John's letters, 2 Peter, and Jude, all dating from the sixties or later, are all preoccupied with problems of internal shortcomings, doctrinal and moral, that were bringing the churches low. That is how the New Testament finishes.

Paul's career gives us a close-up of this situation. Once a rabbi and head of the Jewish inquisition against Christians, he became after his conversion a master evangelist and church planter, and his earlier letters reflect eager hope in God regarding the future spread of the gospel. But his letters to junior pastors Timothy and Titus, written right at the end of his life, are extremely dark: the churches are infected with bad theology and ethical error accompanying it, and Paul expects the bad times to get worse. That is how Paul's career finished. It was a far cry from the glory days of the first two missionary journeys.

A latter-day illustration of downslide from the mountaintop was the experience of Jonathan Edwards, the great theologian and pastoral evangelist who saw revival in his own church in Northampton, New England, in 1735 and again in 1740, at the time of the Great Awakening. His prestige was enormous; he was a recognized authority on matters of theology and spiritual life, and the foremost defender of the Awakening into the bargain. You would not have expected that within a few years of the Awakening his congregation would dismiss him for the biblical line he took on a discipline question (admission to the Lord's Supper) that had social implications. But that is what they did, and Edwards became an obscure frontier missionary as a result. That was how his career finished (for though at the time of his death he had been designated president of Princeton, he had not yet taken office). The Northampton congregation had clearly declined from the quality it had shown during the revivals.

Nehemiah 13 testifies similarly to spiritual decline from a spiritual "high." We have followed Nehemiah through the story of the Jerusalem revival, the "binding agreement" (9:38), and the dedication of the walls. We now note the firm undertaking and detailed arrangements regarding support for the Levites and other temple functionaries. 12:47, which Nehemiah perhaps extracted from temple records, implies that he in person masterminded and enforced all this: "So in the days of . . . Nehemiah [a twelve-year governorship], all Israel contributed the daily portions for the singers and gatekeepers. They also set aside the portion for the other Levites, and the Levites set aside the portion for the descendants of Aaron [i.e., the priests]." But when Nehemiah, having gone back to Susa at the end of his twelve years, returned to Jerusalem at his own request (13:6-7) for a second spell as governor, he found that on four points of the "binding agreement" Israel had lapsed: the temple had been desecrated; tithes had dried up; commerce had encroached on Sabbath observance; and mixed marriages had established themselves once more. So now we read of Nehemiah taking executive action to get things in shape all over again. "If on his first visit he had been a whirlwind," writes Kidner, "on his second he was all fire and earthquake to a city that had settled down in his absence to a comfortable compromise with the gentile world."[2]

It had been perhaps twenty years since the original commitments were made (that is the common guess; Nehemiah does not tell us how long he was at Susa before his second stint began); thus the community had had plenty of time to drift away from the sense it once had of their importance. The memory of the mountaintop experience was no longer vivid, and zeal for God's praise and glory was no longer a driving force. It is, however, likely that Malachi's indictment of shoddy worship (Mal. 1:6-14), a corrupt priesthood (2:1-9), marriage with foreigners (2:10-16), and non-payment of the tithe (3:6-12) was delivered during the years of Nehemiah's absence, so that the people had no excuse at all for the apathy expressed by their continued drift on these matters. Then Nehemiah's fury at the situation he found becomes more explicable, as does also the intensity of his distress at it. For him it was indeed back to square one, and a very sad experience because his high hopes of Israel's fidelity were now dashed. (This, be it said, is an experience with which pastors of churches soon become familiar.)

WORLDLINESS

Second: *conformity to the world is a constant snare to the church.*

Israel's lapses, as recorded both here and elsewhere in the Old Testament, afford vivid illustrations of this truth, about which the New Testament has much to say. The New Testament writers regularly speak of the world in a human and cultural sense, meaning society organized apart from God and against God, and they see the world as always trying to squeeze

Christians individually and the church corporately into its own mold—the mold, that is, of the predominant preconceptions, prejudices, behavior patterns, and styles of life of the particular time and place in which God's people find themselves. The church is the body of Christ, called under the leadership of Jesus, its head, to permeate and purify society and inject God's values, which are the true human values, into its life. Christ wills thus to transform culture through the church's agency. But Satan's empire (that is, pagan and secular ideologies and the communities that embrace them) strikes back, and the conflict is continuous.

Of the church in the world it has been said that while the place for the ship is in the sea, it can only mean disaster when the sea gets into the ship, and this is the truth. Sub-Christian bilge is always seeping into the church and needs to be pumped out; sometimes, too, a battening down of hatchways is needed to prevent the vessel's being swamped by this or that inundation. When God's people cease to be on watch against the world, they are already in its grip, and continuous weakening is all that can be expected as long as this negligence lasts. Meantime, worldly-mindedness, thus induced, will be leading to broken vows and broken lives. The history of Israel makes this plain.

The story here is familiar and depressing. At Sinai the people vowed loyalty to the Lord, and almost immediately broke their vow by orgiastic worship of the golden calf according to a familiar pagan pattern. In the Promised Land there was a seemingly endless flow of similar lapses, leading finally to God's judgments of overthrow and exile. Under Nehemiah's leadership the families of the returned exiles had vowed to tithe and contribute supplies for the maintenance of the temple and its staff, to sanctify the Sabbath, and to cut out mixed marriages (10:30-39). But now it appears that the commercial and diplomatic gains of trading on the Sabbath, marrying foreigners, kowtowing to Tobiah, and limiting donations to the temple for fear of ending up impoverished were throttling all thoughts of what the vows they had taken had actually bound them to do. (For a modern parallel, think of the self-serving reasons that people give, even Christian people, for forgetting the exclusive commitment involved in their marriage vows.)

The old paths of unfaithfulness were being followed once more. The world's values were taking precedence, self-interest was in the saddle, and there in Jerusalem, the Old Testament type and emblem of the Christian church, God was being dishonored afresh. That was tragic, just as it is tragic when counterparts to Israel's commercialism, materialism, unholy diplomacy, self-seeking, and indifference to God's glory appear in Christian congregations today. But as then, so now the Lord's people are under constant pressure to behave in the world's way. Christians are called to be separated to God and therefore different from others in their way of life, just as Israel was; but the call constantly goes unheard, or at least unheeded, just as it did in Nehemiah's time.

DISCIPLINE

Third: *discipline is a constant need in the church.*

I know that the word "discipline," in a church context, conveys to many minds nothing more than the idea of harsh judicial processes; but I use it in its historic Christian sense, which is much broader and has a different focus. It is the English form of the Latin *disciplina*, from a verb that means "to learn," and it signifies the process of educating and training whereby children become wise and mature adults. Learning through the educator's direction is the basic idea, and the correcting of error only comes into it as a means of directing to what is true and good. Coaches in sports harp on what one does wrong in order to get one into the habit of doing things right, and a primary reason why punitive discipline—admonition, barring from the Lord's Table, and disfellowshipping (or excommunication, as disfellowshipping has traditionally been called)—has to be practiced in the church is to lead erring souls to repent and forsake what was wrong in their lives. So discipline should be seen as essentially educational and pastoral rather than as essentially judicial and retributive. It is a matter of putting people on the right track rather than of memorializing the fact that they were once on the wrong one.

Chapter 13 shows us Nehemiah practicing the negative side of discipline. He threw Tobiah's furniture out of the temple (13:8); he rebuked officials, nobles, and heads of families for what they had allowed, in one instance actually coming to blows with the offenders and pulling out their hair (13:11, 17, 25); he threatened Sabbath traders (13:15, 21); he "drove . . . away" ("chased" was the older and more vivid translation) the priest who was Sanballat's son-in-law—in other words, forced him to stop officiating and to leave the city (13:28); and he purified the temple, Levites, and priests (13:9, 22, 30). The positive side of discipline—namely, promoting right thinking and living—was, however, his main concern throughout. He knew that accepting disorder as if it were order and neglecting corrective discipline that would set things truly straight robs God of his glory not only today but tomorrow too.

As neglect of family discipline both spoils children now and jeopardizes their future by making immature and willful adults out of them, so neglect of church discipline produces immature and willful Christians and so guarantees instability in the church of the next generation. The well-being of tomorrow's church is directly linked with the discipline we exercise in the church today. Pastors dare not forget this. Nehemiah's eye was on the future; he wanted to ensure that temple support would never fail again, and that the rest of the "binding agreement" of twenty years earlier

would be observed also. This was strategic planning, far-seeing and statesmanlike. Pastors, take note!

We are now to look in detail at the three disciplinary
episodes that Nehemiah records. We shall watch him in
forthright action for the sanctifying of the sanctuary, the safeguarding of the Sabbath, and the hallowing of home life in
Jerusalem. As he saw it, the worship, the piety, and the
future existence of the restored nation were at risk, and the
firm action that he took seemed to him wholly necessary to
ward off the dangers. The narrative itself is the closing section of Nehemiah's personal memoirs and is written in the
same style as chapters 1–6, with a prayer rounding off each
unit of the story. A further glance at Nehemiah himself will
tune us in to it. Three questions about him pose themselves
as we run our eye over the tale he tells.

AN AGING MAN

First, what should we say about Nehemiah's *age*? How old
was he when he came back to Jerusalem? He nowhere mentions his age, but he would hardly have been appointed governor in the first place had he been less than forty, and that
means that chapter 13 finds him not far from sixty, give or
take a few years. He was thus approaching the end of his
career and was at a point where consolidation of work pre-
viously done naturally and rightly seems important. This,
perhaps, was why he asked Artaxerxes to give him a second
spell as governor (13:6-7).

AN ANGRY MAN

Second, what should we say about Nehemiah's *attitudes*? In
these stories of disciplinary action he comes on exceedingly
strong. He tells us straight out that he was angry (13:8, 21,
25). He was certainly judgmental ("the evil thing," 13:7;
"this wicked thing," 13:17; "all this terrible wickedness,"

13:27). He acted autocratically (which, of course, as governor he was entitled to do), and the "I" becomes rather obtrusive: "I . . . threw . . . out [13:8] . . . I gave orders [13:9] . . . I rebuked [13:11] . . . I called them together [13:11] . . . I put . . . in charge [13:13] . . . I warned [13:15] . . . I ordered [13:19] . . . I stationed [13:19] . . . I warned [13:21] . . . I commanded [13:22] . . . I rebuked . . . called curses down on them . . . beat some . . . pulled out their hair . . . made them take an oath [13:25] . . . I drove him away [13:28] . . . I purified the priests and the Levites [13:30]." Is this anything more than the bad temper and short fuse that tend to mark advancing age? Has not Nehemiah become what we would describe as a difficult old man? Certainly the attitudes he parades (the word is not too strong) require discussion.

What we must bear in mind here, however, is that the conventions and expectations of our smooth post-Christian, relativistic, secular, amoral Western culture are not necessarily in line with the truth and wisdom of God. Any embarrassment we might feel at Nehemiah's forthrightness could be a sign of our own spiritual and moral limitations rather than his. Was it a weakness that in Nehemiah's code of conduct the modern *shibboleth*, "thou shalt be *nice*" seems to have had no place, while "thou shalt be *faithful to God* and *zealous for God*" was evidently basic to it? Would Moses, David, Jesus, or Paul ever have qualified as "Mr. Nice Guy"? The assumption, so common today, that niceness is of the essence of goodness needs to be exploded. Nehemiah should not be criticized for thinking that there are more important things in life than being nice.

If, now, we have a problem with Nehemiah's anger, we should realize that it was a deep feeling of outrage that expressed not self-absorbed resentment nor personal hostility, but the anguish of a heart that longed for God's glory and hated—the word is not too strong—all that obscured and obstructed it. It was, in other words, anger at the situation itself. Jesus showed similar feelings at Lazarus' tomb, where we read that when he saw the weeping mourners he was "*outraged* in spirit" (Jn. 11:33, 38). (The translation is lexically certain, though English versions have softened it to "he groaned," "he sighed," "he was deeply touched," or, as in NIV, "he was deeply moved," thus cutting out the element of anger that is central to the meaning of the Greek word.) Jesus was angry, as the context shows, both at the devastation that sin and death work in human lives and at the unbelief that mourns bereavement despairingly, without any hope of resurrection. And the reason for his anger was not simply his distress at the distresses of others, but basically his awareness that unbelieving responses to death cannot but displease his Heavenly Father. And Nehemiah was angry because in Jerusalem convictions had dimmed, faithfulness had failed, worldliness had invaded, and spiritual ruin was now in progress. Zeal for God's house was eating Nehemiah up, just as later it was to eat Jesus up (Jn. 2:17). Jesus' anger at spiritual degeneration was to lead him to cleanse the temple; Nehemiah's comparable anger led him to cleanse not only the temple but the whole city, as we shall now see.

And if Nehemiah upsets us by seeming to be a judgmental egoist, we should remember that he believed in the absolutes of divine revelation and the reality of God's judgments with a robustness that few nowadays match. Belief in absolutes is out of fashion in the West; relativism and pluralism have become "politically correct" pollutions of the cultural air we breathe, and any affirmation of what purports to be universal truth is thought of as bad manners, if not worse. Before me as I write is a letter that begins: "Our children no longer live in a culture that teaches an objective standard for right and wrong. Truth is a matter of taste; morality has been replaced by individual preference." That is tragically true; and in such a culture the passing of judgments about how others lapse from what we hold to be true and right will always seem judgmental (that is, judging to excess, perversely and unhealthily).

So if we find in ourselves the feeling that Nehemiah was judgmental, we need to check to ensure that we are not simply reflecting the prejudices of the corrupt and corrupting culture of which we are part. We should remind ourselves that relativism and pluralism are marks of cultural decadence, and whatever else may be said about Nehemiah's Jerusalem it was not decadent in the modern manner. In homes where parents seek to teach their children Christian moral standards and to shape their character in line with them, many judgments are passed, and necessarily so; and in the Jerusalem that Nehemiah was trying to mold into a truly God-fearing community the same need for corrective judgment was present. And it is not egoism when a leader insists on things that are in the Bible (in Nehemiah's case, in the Law of Moses), things to which the people whom he judges and admonishes are already formally pledged, and from which they should never have drifted away. So far from being egoism, this is leadership and true pastoral discipline and a building up of the church.

A PRAYING HEART

Third, what should we say about Nehemiah's *appeals* to God—the four brief prayers, each with the invocation "O my God," that punctuate the narrative at verses 14, 22, 29 and 31, three asking God to remember Nehemiah in mercy and one asking him to remember Eliashib's family for judgment?

The basic perspective for understanding these prayers was sketched out earlier. Nehemiah consciously lives, as all the regenerate do, by faith in God's grace—"O my God . . . show mercy to me according to your great love" (13:22);

"remember me with favor, O my God" (13:31, Nehemiah's sign-off line). Only one who lives in dependent personal trust can speak of "my" God. "My" here is the language of covenant, as in "my husband" or "my wife," and signifies, not ownership or control (perish the thought), but sincerity of devotion and reliance—"you are my *God*, for whom, with whom, and through whom I now live." It is most significant that in Nehemiah's memoirs Israel's God is "*my* God" constantly, right up to the very last words.

Again, Nehemiah is consciously committed to God's cause and is wholehearted and thoroughgoing—"flat out," as we might say—in fulfilling the responsibilities God gives him. He does not fear to bring his actions before God for assessment, for he is in touch with his heart and knows what his purpose and motive were—whom, in other words, he was seeking to honor and please. Putting it in New Testament terms, Nehemiah does not pray about his achievements vaingloriously, like the Pharisee in the parable (Lk. 18:10-14), but filially, as a child to a parent. For children to want their father to know what they have done for him, and so to go to him and tell him about it, is natural and not wrong; and the filial instinct of the regenerate constantly moves them to behave this way with their Heavenly Father, just as Jesus' filial nature once moved him to pray: "I have brought you glory on earth by completing the work you gave me to do. And now, Father, glorify me . . ." (Jn. 17:4-5). We should not wonder, then, when in similar fashion Nehemiah prays, "Remember me for this, O my God, and do not blot out what I have so faithfully done for the house of my God and its services" (13:14); "remember me for this also" (13:22). He means: think of me, and know me, as the person who did these things in your interest, whatever the cost was in terms of my discomfort; be aware of my loyal exertions in your cause.

Finally, Nehemiah hands over to God for judgment

those who made themselves enemies of God by their impiety. "Remember them, O my God, because they defiled the priestly office and the covenant of the priesthood and of the Levites" (13:29). He means: I look to for you to deal with them as you see fit.

Nehemiah's prayers reflect both the man and the situation. "They reveal to us the heart of a man continually under pressure in the lonely struggle against evil. They also reflect a man who walks in a moment-by-moment awareness of God. Finally they reflect a man for whom the highest accolade is . . . God's smile of approval, an attitude which is surely an effective defense against spiritual pride."[3] As for Nehemiah's situation, it was, as we have seen, one of spiritual degeneration and harrowing disappointment, in which great effort was now required to remove evils that should never have been there at all. I quote again from Kipling's *If*:

> *If you can bear to hear the truth you've spoken*
> *Twisted by knaves to make a trap for fools,*
> *Or watch the things you gave your life to broken*
> *And stoop and build 'em up with worn out tools . . .*
> *you'll be a Man, my son!*

These lines pinpoint very well the pressures that were on Nehemiah in his second term, and we can imagine what temptations to pessimistic hopelessness assailed him as he worked out what steps were needed to restore Jerusalem's reformation, and then addressed himself to the task. The violence we see in his restorative words and acts, we may be sure, was calculated; he was being as emphatic as he knew he had to be to bring about the desired result. Gentler procedures would not have sufficed.

What we meet in this chapter, then, is not an old man in a hurry, nor a petulant man venting his hurt feelings on everyone within reach, but a humble man of prayerful purpose stooping and building up again what had been broken, and thereby showing himself a Man in Kipling's sense. Viewed in this way, the chapter is a true climax to the book.

THE SANCTUARY SANCTIFIED

Tobiah, as we noted (6:17-19), was tied into Jerusalem's social and political establishment and had connections with various key people who would do him favors. One such favor was the action of Eliashib the high priest in handing over to him a temple storeroom, "the size of a small warehouse,"[4] to be his city apartment and headquarters. Storerooms were intended to provide temporary accommodation for priests, singers, and gatekeepers during their spells of temple duty (10:39), but the layman Tobiah had no business in the temple at all. Nehemiah, scandalized at Eliashib's arrangement, "threw all Tobiah's household goods out of the room" (13:8). This need only mean that he gave the orders to have this done; but it sounds as if he did it both personally, to make a public gesture of it, and violently, to show how outrageous Tobiah's intrusion had been. So we may imagine pieces of furniture, the smaller ones at any rate, flying out of the door as Nehemiah ceremonially threw them ("threw" is the literal meaning of the verb); and it may be that Tobiah, probably by now a dignified senior citizen, had to stand there spluttering while this strong-arm eviction went on. Thus the room was cleared; then all the temple storerooms were purified, as if Tobiah's presence in one had defiled them all—"and then I put back into them the equipment of the house of God, with the grain offerings and the incense" (13:9).

One reason, evidently, why Eliashib had been happy to allocate a storeroom to Tobiah was that grain offerings—that is, the tithes of grain—had not been coming in in any quantity, so that the storage areas for them were not all needed. The falling-off of tithes had meant that the Levites and temple musicians, whom the tithes were meant to support, had had to leave their appointed place of service in Jerusalem to farm their small holdings outside the city, lest they starve. Now, however, Nehemiah cracked the whip; the tithes came in once more from "all Judah [that is, Jerusalem and the country round]"; and Nehemiah put "trustworthy" men in charge of storage and distribution to the singers and Levites. Thus the temple and its affairs were put back in order (13:10-14), according to the terms of the "binding agreement" (10:37-39; cf. 9:38).

The ceremonial defilement of the temple storerooms resulting from the unauthorized residence of the self-serving schemer Tobiah in one of them is a vivid picture of the moral defilement that comes from misuse of powers and resources in the life of churches and Christians—both described by Paul as God's temple, indwelt by the Holy Spirit (see 1 Cor. 3:16-17; 6:19). Besetting sins, unhallowed relationships, the self-serving pursuit of pleasure, profit, power, or position, unconcern about pleasing and glorifying God, and any pattern of action that in any way undermines obedience to God's written Word and fidelity to the Christ of the Scriptures has a defiling effect in God's sight, of which healthy consciences will be aware. As it was necessary to throw Tobiah out of the temple at Jerusalem long ago, so sinful acts and ways must be repented of, renounced, and given up today; and as it was necessary to enforce the specifics of the law of worship in Nehemiah's time, so it is necessary that the disciplines of discipleship be relearned in our time.

And just as it was not unsuitable for Nehemiah and Jesus to be angry at the evil which they sought to cast out of the temple, so it will not be unsuitable for us to let ourselves feel anger at the evil in our hearts, in our lives, and in our surroundings as we seek to negate and repel it by the help of our God. If we cannot feel anger at sin, there is something wrong with us; and if we could be more angry at sin, we should be less indulgent towards it.

THE SABBATH SAFEGUARDED

The Sabbath that God required Israel to observe was a day of abstinence from whatever the work was that had filled the previous six days. In general, the Sabbath was a sign that all our time must be seen as a gift from God, to be used as he directs; in particular, it was a day for remembering and celebrating the work of God in both creation and redemption. The way to honor God in Sabbath-keeping was declared to the people by God himself through Isaiah:

> *"If you keep your feet from breaking the Sabbath*
> *and from doing as you please on my holy day,*
> *if you call the Sabbath a delight*
> *and the LORD's holy day honorable,*
> *and if you honor it by not going your own way*
> *and not doing as you please or speaking idle words,*
> *then you will find your joy in the LORD,*
> *and I will cause you to ride on the heights of the land*
> *and to feast on the inheritance of your father Jacob."*
> *The mouth of the LORD has spoken.*
>
> (58:13-14)

It was as if God said: "Observe the fourth commandment faithfully, honor and enjoy the day of rest and worship that I prescribe for you, and I will bless and honor you. But if you moan and groan about the need for this observance, and try to evade it, your story will be very different. And remember that keeping this commandment begins with an attitude of heart—one that expects an obedient Sabbath to be not dreary but delightful, because of the fellowship with me, your God, that it furthers." This is certainly the wavelength to which

Nehemiah was tuned when he addressed the question of how the Sabbath should be kept in Jerusalem (13:15-22).

Nehemiah forbade Sabbath markets, which were in full swing when he arrived, with Jews and non-Jews ("men from Tyre") equally involved. He ordered the city gates closed from the evening before the Sabbath to the morning after, and warned off those who camped before the gates overnight on the Sabbath so they could begin business first thing next day. He explained to the nobles (the trend-setters in the community) why they must use their influence to oppose Sabbath trading rather than to encourage it. "Didn't your forefathers do the same things [trade on the Sabbath], so that our God brought all this calamity [the exile and its aftermath] upon us and upon this city? Now you are stirring up more wrath against Israel by desecrating the Sabbath" (13:18). Do we believe in a God who punishes his own people when they fail to honor him by obedience, but instead profane that which to him is precious? Nehemiah did, and both Testaments consistently say the same. The writer to the Hebrews is quoting and expounding Proverbs 3:12 when he declares, "'The Lord disciplines those he loves, and he punishes everyone he accepts as a son' . . . human fathers . . . disciplined us and we respected them for it. . . . God disciplines us for our good, that we may share in his holiness" (Heb. 12:6, 9-10). It was within this frame of reference, with God's displeasure and discipline in his mind, that Nehemiah insisted on restoring the Sabbath observance that was promised in the "binding agreement" (9:38), from which Jerusalem had so signally lapsed.

Whether the day that the New Testament calls the Lord's day, the first day of the week when Christians meet for worship (Acts 20:7; 1 Cor. 16:2; Rev. 1:10), should be spoken of as the Christian Sabbath or not is a disputed question among Bible-believers,[5] and I shall not try to decide it here. The point of contemporary application that I wish to make applies whichever of these views you take. It is this: the Lord's day is God's gift to us for the health of our souls and of the souls of others, and we must appreciate, honor, and use it accordingly. It is a day of spiritual opportunity, because it is the day of united worship; it is in the worship together of his people that God specially makes himself known. The Puritans, who used to call the Lord's day "the market-day of the soul," the high spot of the week, believed that a well-spent Lord's day was a necessary preparation for the six days' work that would then follow, and that Christians simply could not afford to treat the day as trivial and reduce it to routine. Do we value the Lord's day in this way, and prepare for it, make the most of it, and take care lest secular concerns encroach upon it, in the way that Nehemiah wanted the Jerusalemites to value and profit from their Sabbaths?

This is a question that many professed Christians need to face. Safeguarding and sanctifying the Lord's day requires of modern Christians ever more clarity of purpose as secularism eats away at Christian public observances and our pagan culture assimilates Sunday more and more completely to being like any other day of the week, thus in effect returning to the paganism of the world to which Christianity first came, and from which Christians were instructed to be distinctively different. In England, a recent campaign against Sunday trading was organized under the slogan, "Keep Sunday Special." That is a fine slogan in countries where the Christian Sunday is part of the cultural inheritance, and "Make Sunday Special" would be a fine slogan anywhere in the world. But we cannot pursue this any further now.

HOME LIFE HALLOWED

"We promise not to give our daughters in marriage to the peoples around us or take their daughters for our sons"

(10:30). So ran the "binding agreement." At the time of its making, racial purity had been a matter of general concern, and the people had "excluded from Israel all who were of foreign descent" (13:3), thus going beyond the Law, which excluded only Ammonites and Moabites. But the zeal for purity of Israelite blood, and for doing everything to please God, which had presumably prompted that exclusivism, had evaporated, and when Nehemiah returned to Jerusalem he found there "men of Judah who had married women from Ashdod, Ammon and Moab" (13:23). The reason may, of course, have been passion, but it is more likely to have been the prudence, if we should call it that, which has its eye on the main chance and marries for money or prestige or some other form of worldly gain. And in some cases Nehemiah found that it was the non-Jewish language that the parents had decided to speak at home, so that their children "did not know how to speak the language of Judah" (13:24). This sent Nehemiah right up in the air: not only because it was the breach of a vow, but because it meant that these children would be unable to share in Israel's worship, or to learn the Law effectively, and so would not be able to pass on Israel's faith to the children that they themselves would have in due course, so that the future spiritual unity of the nation would be at risk.

Seeing this very clearly, and not liking what he saw, Nehemiah called a meeting, apparently, at which he made a speech to Jewish men who had broken the "binding agreement" in this way, reminding them of Solomon's fall—"led into sin by foreign women"—and requiring them to swear in God's name not to effect any more mixed marriages, either by taking foreign brides "for your sons or for yourselves" or by marrying their daughters to foreign males. Ezra, many years before, had led in breaking up mixed marriages as being wholly contrary to God's will (Ezra 9–10). Nehemiah did not go so far, but settled for their non-prolif-

eration and non-recurrence. This was a statesmanlike compromise. Nehemiah, wisely, did not want to disrupt the
community more than necessary; so he simply demanded a
sworn undertaking that no more mixed marriages would
take place.

To be sure, he did this on the basis of first making an
example of some notorious offenders. "I beat some of the
men and pulled out their hair." This need only mean that in
his role as head of the judiciary, which as governor he was,
he ordered floggings according to the prescription of
Deuteronomy 25:1-3 and imposed sentences of shaving the
head, recalling perhaps in his sentencing speech how once
Ezra had torn out his own hair (Ezra 9:3) over the evil of
mixed marriages, though it could of course mean that he
inflicted this punitive violence on their persons himself.
And then he "drove [Eliashib's grandson] away from me"—
presumably by peremptory decree of banishment, though
"chased" is the literal meaning and the possibility of a furious Nehemiah running the man out of the room or the
building they were in cannot be excluded. In any case,
Nehemiah's form of words shows that he claims responsibility for what was done, is in retrospect glad that he made it
happen, and wants us to see it as an appropriate and effective
expression of his reforming zeal and pastoral purpose—
which surely it was.

We need not suppose that Nehemiah enjoyed having to
do any of these things. We may be sure that he would much
rather not have had to go back to square one and re-reform
Israel's already deformed reformation in this way. But life is
full of unwelcome necessities for everyone, and for none
more so than for pastoral leaders in God's church, who constantly need Nehemiah's combination of zeal for God and
care for people so as to deal with the disorders that emerge.
Sin and Satan will never stop corrupting belief and behavior
within the community that bears God's name; disorders,

perversities, and confusions are therefore to be expected, and those who guide the community must not be daunted at finding themselves compelled to deal with the same problems and deviations again and again, over and above the new ones that keep appearing. Nehemiah, with his passion for faithfulness and his prayerful persistence in well-doing, is a model for us here.

Thoughtful pastoral leaders, like Nehemiah, always focus on families and family life, for the family is the first and most basic form of human community. Family nurture, for better or for worse, goes deeper into children than any form of nurture from elsewhere, and the biblical ideal is that families should be the composite units out of which each church is built. Godliness is to be modeled in the family, and faith passed on there. Everywhere in today's Western world, and to some extent in urban communities everywhere on the face of the globe, family life is being weakened and undermined by pressures of various sorts, and this is likely to get worse. So the need to work as Nehemiah worked to keep family life strong, godly, and wholesome is great, and all who strategize and minister to spread God's kingdom today and tomorrow must make families and home life a matter of prime concern.

DO WHAT YOU CAN

"She did what she could," said Jesus of the woman who honored him by pouring her entire jar of precious nard ointment over him, holding none of it back; "she has done a beautiful thing to me" (Mk. 14:8, 6). Nehemiah also did what he could, using his brains, creativity, strength of mind and body, position and privilege, wisdom and wealth up to the limit in order to honor God, build up his people, and advance his praise in Jerusalem. Recent studies of Nehemiah have profiled him as an example of leadership,[6] and this is not wrong;

but I would like our final view of him, as we take our leave of his book, to center upon the example he set of persevering faithfulness as such—a quality that followers need to cultivate no less than leaders. Certainly he excelled as one of God's public figures, and we may well endorse, three hundred years after, the verdict of Matthew Henry, the Puritan commentator, who wrote:

> In my esteem, Ezra . . . and Nehemiah . . . though neither of them ever wore a crown, commanded an army, conquered any country, or were famed for philosophy or oratory, yet both of them, being pious praying men, and very serviceable in their day to the church of God and the interests of religion, were really greater men . . . not only than any of the Roman consuls or dictators, but than Xenophon, or Demosthenes, or Plato himself, who lived at the same time, the bright ornaments of Greece.[7]

But in my esteem Nehemiah stands out even more as one of God's personal friends, who blesses me most by letting me, so to speak, hear his heart of faith beating as he tells me of the tasks he tackled and the obstacles he surmounted, and the way he refused to be discouraged when he had, in effect, to go back to the beginning and start again.

It seems clear that this is the way he himself hoped to come across as he put his memoirs into final shape; for he spends chapter 1 telling us the contents of the prayer that he and others first made for Jerusalem, the prayer in answer to which, as he saw it, his entire ministry at Jerusalem unfolded; and he makes a point of inserting for us many windows into his prayer life as he goes along; and his exit line in chapter 13 is a final prayer for himself as he looks back over his life of service and the way God used him in rebuilding the walls, rebuilding the community, and then of necessity laboring to rebuild (or should we say, re-rebuild?) what he rebuilt before—"Remember me with favor, O my God" (13:31)—"remember me, O my God, for good," as the older versions have it. On these words the comment of Matthew Henry can hardly be bettered:

> The best services done for the public have sometimes been forgotten by those for whom they were done (Eccl. ix.15); therefore Nehemiah refers himself to God, to recompense him, takes him for his Pay-master, and then doubts not but he shall be well paid. This may well be the summary of our petitions, we need no more to make us happy than this, *Remember me, O my God, for good.*

It is for us, then, to learn from Nehemiah to do what we can for our God, his cause, and his church, so fulfilling our calling as Christian disciples, whom Jesus declares to be his personal friends (Jn. 15:13-15). Those who live under grace should overflow with gratitude, and that gratitude should show itself by acts of loyalty and love. It is, then, for us to spend and be spent in serving others for our Lord's sake. And thus we may make Nehemiah's last prayer our own and verify in experience Kidner's dictum, "To hear God's 'Well done' is the most . . . cleansing of ambitions." [8]

Nearly two centuries ago, Charles Simeon had hanging in his study at King's College, Cambridge, a portrait of Henry Martyn, his protégé, a pioneer missionary who gave his life in service to the Muslim world. Simeon would sometimes tell visitors that the businesslike expression on Martyn's face in the portrait came as a message to him every time he looked at it, reminding him of the importance of not frittering life away in trifling pursuits. Then he would wag his finger at the portrait and say, in front of his visitors, playfully yet seriously, as it were to Martyn, to himself, and to his Lord, "And I won't trifle—I won't trifle."

Nehemiah's verbal self-portrait carries a similar message and calls for a similar response from Christian believers today. If we cannot do for Christ and his church all that we would, let us at least not trifle, but, like Nehemiah, do all that we can.

Epilogue:
Two Imposters

The title phrase for this closing reflection comes from a brilliant little poem about maturity, from which I have taken two quotes already—Rudyard Kipling's *If*. Here are the relevant lines:

> *If you can dream—and not make dreams your master;*
> *If you can think—and not make thoughts your aim;*
> *If you can meet with Triumph and Disaster*
> *And treat those two imposters just the same . . .*

Then, says Kipling eventually, "you'll be a Man, my son!" Though not an avowedly Christian statement, this poem is full of biblical wisdom, and nowhere more so than in the half-verse quoted above. Here Kipling tells us that the mature person will be able to imagine new possibilities, yet without losing touch with reality; he will be able to conceptualize and argue and debate, yet without becoming a doctrinaire theorist; and beyond that he will view any present success and any present collapse of his projects as delusive to a degree, looking like what they are not, and therefore he will take them in stride as simply episodes in the unfolding tapestry of a purposeful life. Moses, David, Paul, and Jesus all illustrate these aspects of maturity beautifully—and so does Nehemiah.

MATURITY

Triumph and Disaster are given initial capitals, as Man is, but no other words in the poem are. I suppose Kipling does that because both come to us as overwhelming experiences presenting themselves as in some sense definitive and final. A moment of conscious triumph makes one feel that after this nothing will really matter; a moment of realized disaster makes one feel that this is the end of everything. But neither feeling is realistic, for neither event is really what it is felt to be. The circumstances of triumph will not last, and the moment of triumph will sooner or later give way to moments of disappointment, strain, frustration, and grief, while the circumstances of disaster will prove to have in them seeds of recovery and new hope. Life in this world under God's providence is like that; it always has been, and always will be; it is so in the Bible, and it remains so as the twentieth century gives way to the twenty-first. The mature person, who is mentally and emotionally an adult as distinct from a child, knows this and does not forget it.

Those who bear responsibility for the welfare of others, whether as spouses, parents, homemakers, teachers, leaders, pastors, organizers, managers, or whatever—and that includes most, if not all, of us—will feel the ups and downs of life more acutely in proportion as more people are involved with us in the events that take place. Nehemiah's sense of triumph at the completing and dedicating of Jerusalem's new wall must have been greatly enhanced by the thought that this was a triumph for the entire nation of which as governor he was leader and head. So, too, his sense of disaster when he discovered on his return to Jerusalem that the revival which was in progress at the time of the dedication had almost completely run into the sand must have been greatly deepened by the thought that this left the whole people spiritually as low, dry, and apathetic as they were before he first arrived there. Yet no doubt it was awareness that this decline could happen, and perhaps news that made him suspect it had happened, that led him to ask Artaxerxes for a second spell as governor (13:6). No doubt, too, he was sure that the God who had taken him to Jerusalem and given him such success in his first term would now give him the strength and stick-to-it-iveness he would need to (Kipling again) "watch the things you gave your life to broken / And stoop and build 'em up with worn out tools." Certainly that strength was given him, and some communal recovery after the disaster of Jerusalem's backsliding did in fact take place. But if Nehemiah ended his days as an old lion, fiercer than in his youth because emotionally worn by his years of unrewarded and unappreciated faithfulness in leadership for God, no one should be surprised. We do not know, of course, whether this is what happened, but some of the rough touches in his book have sometimes been thought to suggest it.

All along, however, Nehemiah's clear-headed, single-minded faithfulness to the job he was called to do, his shrewd wisdom, his willingness to speak out, take a lead, cross swords with powerful people, and stand the heat in the kitchen, plus his sustained confidence that his God would see him through, were utterly admirable. A hundred years ago the Anglican Bishop John Charles Ryle was described as a man of granite with the heart of a child, and that description fits Nehemiah too. The tone of Nehemiah's memoirs shows that behind his bold forthrightness was humility; behind his cool resilience in the cold war that Sanballat and Tobiah waged against him was faith; behind his pep-talks to the people to keep them rebuilding first the wall and then their national life was love, which biblically is to be measured not by what one says to people, but by what one does for them (see 1 Jn. 3:16-18; Neh. 5:19); behind the tensions and anxieties of his pioneering leadership was joy—the joy of knowing and serving Israel's Lord, and of seeing him work in power and grace (8:10); and behind

Nehemiah's prayers for vindication was the integrity that abandons sin as soon as it is realized to be sin (5:10) and that always refuses to transgress God's Law for any consideration whatever, even life itself (6:11).

In all these respects Nehemiah stands before us as a magnificent model of responsible leadership rooted in radical godliness. He and Moses are often bracketed together as the first and second founders of Israel's national life; in personal stature also they appear very close to each other, as great men by any standards, and in particular here as great men of God.

At the close of *If* Kipling notes one last element needed for maturity as follows:

> *If you can fill the unforgiving minute*
> *With sixty seconds' worth of distance run—*
> *Yours is the earth and everything in it,*
> *And—which is more—you'll be a Man, my son!*

The thought is vivid and clear. Minutes are "unforgiving" because they will not pause for us or return for us; so we must learn to make the most of each one as it goes by. Goal-oriented energy is required for this: hence "distance *run*." "Yours is the earth" is a letdown; it is a secular platitude of nineteenth-century type, euphoric but hollow, implying that effort always brings prosperity, which it does not. But the insight that maturity—being a Man—is distinct from, and more important than, winding up wealthy takes Kipling out on a high. All cultures know, deep down, that personal maturity is a supreme value, but for none is this truth truer than for followers of the Man of Galilee, whose calling it is to seek from their Saviour moral transformation into his likeness. Energetic purposefulness is, however, central to that likeness, just as it is central to the example set us by Moses and Nehemiah. And there is a sense, distinct from what Kipling had in mind, in which diligent servants of God do inherit the earth, but we cannot go into that now. Suffice it to underline the truth we see instanced in Nehemiah, as in Jesus, that purposeful energy with persistent integrity is essential to the Christlike personal maturity at which we all should aim.

Nehemiah, then, is a man to admire and to imitate—but be careful! The theme of imitating Bible characters is often mishandled. Bryan Chapell has written of the "deadly Be's" ("killer Be's" would have been more vivid), of which the first is sermons that require us to "be like" some figure in the Scripture story. Such sermons summon us to a treadmill life of perpetual role-play that is bound in the end to prove self-defeating, for, as Chapell rightly comments: "Simply telling people to imitate godliness in another without reminding them that anything more than outward conformity must come from God forces them either to despair of spiritual transformation or to deny its need."[1] This is not a road down which to go, and when I speak of imitating Nehemiah I have in mind something quite different: namely, following the example of his faith and relationship with God.

What will that mean for us? Whoever and whatever we are, however we are placed and wherever we serve, it will mean at least the following: attention to the Scriptures in order to find God's will; appropriation of God in covenant as "my God" (which for Christians also means appropriation of Jesus Christ as "my Saviour and Lord"); devotion in the form of prayers of petition, celebration, sometimes desperation, and perhaps even imprecation when we find ourselves up against evil; preparation to deal with the two imposters, Triumph and Disaster, both of which are going to invade our lives from time to time; expectation of help and deliverance in answer to prayer; motivation to seek God's glory by practicing full-scale obedience to him; and a passion for the kind of stubborn faithfulness that is resolved to honor God and show forth his praise through thick and thin. Imitating Nehemiah will mean anchoring our souls in the sentiments of Psalm 26, which for all we know might have been one of his favorites:

> *Vindicate me, O LORD,*
> *for I have led a blameless life;*
> *I have trusted in the LORD*
> *without wavering.*
> *Test me, O LORD, and try me,*
> *examine my heart and my mind,*
> *for your love is ever before me,*
> *and I walk continually in your truth. . . .*
> *I wash my hands in innocence,*
> *and go about your altar, O LORD,*
> *proclaiming aloud your praise*
> *and telling of all your wonderful deeds.*
> *I love the house where you live, O LORD,*
> *the place where your glory dwells.*
> *Do not take away my soul along with sinners,*
> *my life with bloodthirsty men . . .*
> *redeem me and be merciful to me.*
> *My feet stand on level ground;*
> *in the great assembly I will praise the LORD.*
> (Ps. 26:1-3, 6-9, 11-12)

The counterpart of Nehemiah in the New Testament era is the Apostle Paul, another human ball of fire with a passion for faithfulness in building up God's church, a passion rooted like Nehemiah's in a life of faith, hope, love, and joy. Like Nehemiah, Paul knew how to deal with the imposters Triumph and Disaster; triumphs seem never to have turned his head, nor disasters led him to give up hope. Like Nehemiah, he saw believing communities that were formed under revival conditions, when God worked through his Word most powerfully, lose momentum and drift; like Nehemiah, he labored hard in prayer and by instruction to get them back into shape. His knowledge of Jesus Christ set him in one sense ahead of Nehemiah, but the covenantal shape and substance of the relationship with God ("*my* God") that both enjoyed was the same, and Paul's words in the last chapter of his last letter may well be cited here to round off our study of his great predecessor. Wrote Paul:

> I have fought the good fight, I have finished the race, I have kept the faith. Now there is in store for me the crown of righteousness, which the Lord, the righteous Judge, will award to me on that day—and not only to me, but also to all who have longed for his appearing. . . . The Lord will rescue me from every evil attack and will bring me safely to his heavenly kingdom. To him be glory for ever and ever. Amen. (2 Tim. 4:7-8, 18)

This spells out in New Testament terms all that is implicit in Nehemiah's sign-off prayer: "Remember me with favor, O my God" (13:31). "We need no more to make us happy than this," was Matthew Henry's comment on that petition. He was right. And nothing better can be desired for this author or his readers than that our fidelity should match Paul's and Nehemiah's to the very end of life, so that we too may in due time enjoy the ultimate and supreme happiness before God's throne that is at the present moment most surely theirs.

SUCCESS?

Would it then be right to describe Nehemiah and Paul as successes in their respective ministries? The question is worth raising as we close, because the passion for success constantly becomes a spiritual problem—really, a lapse into idolatry—in the lives of God's servants today. To want to succeed in things that matter is of course natural, and not wrong in itself, but to feel that one must at all costs be able to project oneself to others as a success is an almost demonized state of mind, from which deliverance is needed. Here, again, as we shall see, Nehemiah, and Paul with him, can help us.

But first let it be said that this success syndrome is an infection that has spread right through the whole Western world, so that its prevalence among Christian people, though distressing, is hardly surprising. The world's idea that everyone, from childhood up, should be able to succeed at all times in measurable ways, and that it is a great disgrace not to, hangs over the Christian community like a pall of acrid smoke; and if the spiritual counterpart of agonized coughing, lung pain, and shortness of breath should result, no one should be surprised. Those who want to become, and in some cases be hired as, Christ's agents in building his church now feel they have to have track records that show them as successes in everything to which they ever put their hand. So the imposters have a field day: anything that in the short term looks like triumph (opposition overcome, obstacles surmounted, expansion encompassed) is equated with personal success, and anything that in the short term looks like disaster (loss of money, status, job, support, or whatever) is seen as failure. Successful-looking performance at all costs becomes the goal, and unreality creeps into people's view of themselves as a result.

On my desk as I write lies a broadsheet for pastors that begins with the banner headline, "How Will I Know When I've Succeeded?" You can see why I read that with mixed feelings. The burden of the broadsheet is that pastors must be pro-active rather than reactive, committed to mission and outreach rather than mere maintenance and marking time, and that for this they need a philosophy of ministry—that is, a thought-out rationale of ends and means. Defined goals, it says, give you direction, generate energy, sustain morale (because now you know where you are going), show you what on a daily basis is really important for you and so deliver you from the tyranny of the merely urgent, facilitate team-building and the eliciting of cooperation and support, and enable you to evaluate how you are doing; and all of that is mostly certainly true and valuable. But we can succeed in reaching goals we have set ourselves and still not know God's verdict on what we have been up to. The fact that I have thus succeeded does not mean that God now necessarily counts me a success.

The problem is that my ideas of success are regularly much more self-serving than I realize, and the self they serve is a sinful, prideful self. Let me be anecdotal for a moment to illustrate this.

When I was young, British, and pagan, I thought the sky was the limit and nothing I wanted to do was beyond me. My dreams ranged from being a star cricketer to a distinguished locomotive engineer to a top comedian, with much bizarre stuff in between. But spectacular success was always part of the dream, and every failure hurt because it punctured my conceit.

When I became a Christian, which happened at university, I had the simplistic zeal you expect of a convert. When I read Charles Finney and D. L. Moody, I loved them (I still do) and absorbed uncritically their boundless and indeed grandiose optimism as to what God can do if only his people are willing to cooperate. For years I went on thinking that spectacular success in one's work for God was the right thing to pray for, and the only sure sign that one was serving the Lord as one should. Most of my conceit, I fear, was still there.

Now I live in Canada and have found that churches, pastors, seminaries, and parachurch agencies throughout North America are mostly playing the numbers game—that is, defining success in terms of numbers of heads counted or added to those that were there before. Church-growth theorists, evangelists, pastors, missionaries, news reporters, and others all speak as if (1) numerical increase is what matters most; (2) numerical increase will surely come if our techniques and procedures are right; (3) numerical increase validates ministries as nothing else does; (4) numerical increase must be everyone's main goal. I detect four unhappy consequences of this.

First, big and growing churches are viewed as far more significant than others.

Second, parachurch specialists who pull in large numbers (evangelists, college and seminary teachers with platform skills, medicine men with traveling seminars, riders on convention circuits, top people in youth movements, full-time authors, and such) are venerated, while hard-working pastors are treated as near-nonentities.

Third, lively laymen and clergy too are constantly being creamed off from the churches to run parachurch ministries, in which, just because they specialize on a relatively narrow front, quicker and more striking results can be expected.

Fourth, many ministers of not-so-bouncy temperament and not-so-flashy gifts return to secular employment in disillusionment and bitterness, concluding that the pastoral life of steady service is a game not worth playing.

In all of this I seem to see a great deal of unmortified pride, either massaged, indulged, and gratified, or wounded, nursed, and mollycoddled. Where quantifiable success is god, pride always grows strong and spreads through the soul as cancer sometimes gallops through the body. Shrinking spiritual stature and growing moral weakness thence result, and in pastoral leaders, especially those who have become sure they are succeeding, the various forms of abuse and exploitation that follow can be horrific. The fruit of nourished pride is invariably bitter. Orienting all Christian action to visible success as its goal, a move which to many moderns seems supremely sensible and businesslike, is thus more a weakness in the church than it is a strength; it is a seedbed both of unspiritual vainglory for the self-rated succeeders and of unspiritual despair for the self-rated failures, and a source of shallowness and superficiality all round. After setting biblically appropriate goals, embracing biblically appropriate means of seeking to realize them, assessing as best we can where we have got to in pursuing them, and making any course corrections that our assessments suggest, the way of health and humility is for us to admit to ourselves that in the final analysis we do not and cannot know the measure of our success as God sees it. Wisdom says: leave success ratings to God, and live your Christianity as a religion of faithfulness rather than an idolatry of achievement.

Some years ago I put some of these thoughts in an article commending a book by Kent and Barbara Hughes titled *Liberating Ministry from the Success Syndrome*—a book that I would like to see made required reading for every pastor and pastoral aspirant. The wily editors retitled my offering "Nothing Fails Like Success" and printed it alongside a paid-for half-column advertising the "Robert Schuller Institute for Successful Church Leadership." I never dared ask them whom they saw as trashing whom, or even whether they noticed what they had done (what looked like wiliness might, after all, have been just goofiness). But I confess that I wanted both to laugh and groan when I saw the page, and thinking back to it I still do. Applauder of pastoral enterprise and goal setting, of church expansion and aggressive evangelism, of evaluation, assessment, and accountability that I am, when spiritual success seems to be pragmatically defined in terms of making programs happen and Christian initiative seems to be market-driven rather than God-focused, I shudder. And it was Nehemiah, as much as anyone, who taught me to do that.

For the truth is that our success in the real business of church-building—not the production of plant and programs, but the shepherd's work of gathering, nurturing, feeding, and guiding those whom Christ pictures as the sheep of his flock—is something that only God is ever in a position to measure. I think of two English congregations, one twice the size of the other, both of which under the influence of liberal theology had become sluggish, complacent, and deeply unspiritual. A robust minister of the gospel was appointed to each. The one serving the small congregation stayed five years; his counterpart in the large congregation stayed ten. Each man spent much of his time trying to change, or at least circumvent, a block of old stagers who did not like their minister, resisted his emphases, and were resolved to see him out. Both left those churches feeling failures, because the opposition had not been dislodged. Both were followed by equally robust evangelicals, who early in their ministry saw the opposition cave in, and both congregations are now outstanding centers of evangelical vitality and joy, having quietly doubled in size since the battle for a pure and powerful gospel was joined. I have no doubt that in the annals of eternity all the seeds of true spiritual success in both places will prove to have been sown by the pioneer, trouble-shooting evangelicals who thought themselves failures, and that their achievement will stand forever as success in the sight of God. But at the time of the successful sowing it was not possible to foresee the subsequent successful reaping, and the years of sowing against entrenched hostility felt in the short term like failure. Such situations are more common than we sometimes allow.

Did Nehemiah at the end of his own public life feel a failure? He might well have. I cannot prove that when he wrote his testimony to the way God had led and used him he felt doubt as to the long-term significance of what he had accomplished; but I know that in his shoes I would have been fearful on that score. What he had seen was a spectacular spiritual revival followed by a drastic spiritual relapse.

Forthright action during his second spell at Jerusalem had put things straight for the time being, but how deep was the people's sense of sin and of their obligation to love the Lord who loved them, and how long the new order—strictly, the renewed order—might last was more than Nehemiah could tell. His chapter 13 is clearly meant to stand as an admonitory testimony against subsequent slippage and a modeling of the sort of loyalty to God that he wanted all Jews to show. Thus it was (and is) a call to faithfulness, and within that frame the wording of the interjected prayer of verse 14 gains new significance. "Remember me for this, O my God," Nehemiah prays, "and do not blot out [from your mind] what I have *so faithfully* done for the house of my God and its services." Nehemiah's passion was for faithfulness; whether he had been appointed to succeed he did not know, but he knew he was called to be faithful to the word of his God in all things. And in this he sets us an example of the spiritual person's mind-set that, please God, we shall never forget.

Something similar should be said about Paul. As we noticed above, he had seen churches born and for a time grow under revival conditions; but by the end of his life zeal was flagging, heresy was flooding in, persecution was starting, and the spiritual sky was darkening in every direction. As in his somber last letter he anticipates his death, he has nothing to say about having been a success, only that, unlike some, "I have fought the good fight, I have finished the race, I have kept the faith" (2 Tim. 4:7). He does not know whether he has been a success or not; all he is sure of is that he has been faithful, holding fast to God's truth and righteousness when others let both go. In this he, like Nehemiah, is a model for us to imitate.

In fact, of course, the long-term effects of both Nehemiah's and Paul's work as shapers of God's people in the life of faith and holiness has been enormous, so that we may truly say, if we want to, that both were outstandingly successful, rising to triumphs and coping with disasters with wonderful wisdom, and marking out paths of godliness in a way that put later generations forever in their debt. But my present point is that, however much success they actually had, their calling was not to success but to faithfulness—and so is ours, whatever our role in the body of Christ. Christ will build his church, using us as he wills, in ways that involve the appearance of triumph and disaster over and over again. Our part is not to let either appearance fool us, but to maintain an unflinching fidelity to the particular tasks and roles we know we have been given to fulfill, all for the honoring and pleasing of the Father, the Son, and the Holy Spirit, who by their joint action are the true agents of the entire building process. Such faithfulness—the grace of zealously keeping on keeping on whether discouraged or encouraged, with a humility that stays constant when encouraged no less than when discouraged—is the final lesson that Nehemiah has to teach us. And it is a lesson that we shall only ever learn through divine help, help that is found by keeping close to Jesus Christ.

The conclusion of the matter then is this: as it is our wisdom to take Nehemiah, veteran of the seeming triumph of the revival and the seeming disaster of the relapse, as our role model in whatever form of service lies at our hand, so it is our wisdom to take Jesus Christ, veteran of the seeming triumph of Palm Sunday and the seeming disaster of Good Friday, as our trainer in Nehemiah-like behavior, and to know that the faithfulness in which he drills us is his own gift to us, through the power of the Holy Spirit. Here is wisdom that we urgently need to take hold of, whoever we are, so that God may be truly glorified in our lives and his church truly built up through our efforts.

Notes

CHAPTER 1: MEET NEHEMIAH

1. John White, *Excellence in Leadership* (Downers Grove, IL: InterVarsity Press, 1986), p. 9ff.
2. J. C. Ryle, *Practical Religion* (London: James Clarke, 1959), p. 130.
3. White, *Excellence in Leadership*, p. 23ff.

CHAPTER 2: CALLED TO SERVE

1. Westminster Confession, X.1.
2. White, *Excellence in Leadership*, p. 37.
3. E. M. Bounds, *Prayer and Praying Men* (Grand Rapids, MI: Baker, n.d.), p. 73ff.

CHAPTER 3: MAN-MANAGEMENT I: GETTING GOING

1. White, *Excellence in Leadership*, p. 61.
2. *Ibid.*, p. 59ff.
3. Quoted by Cyril J. Barber, *Nehemiah and the Dynamics of Effective Leadership* (Neptune, NJ: Loizeaux Brothers, 1976), p. 19.
4. James Montgomery Boice, *Nehemiah: Learning to Lead* (Old Tappan, NJ: Revell, 1990), p. 22, quoting Charles R. Swindoll, *Hand Me Another Brick* (Nashville: Thomas Nelson, 1978), p. 30.
5. A plan of the walls and gates of Jerusalem can be found in Derek Kidner, *Ezra and Nehemiah* (Leicester: Inter-Varsity Press, 1979), p. 85, and in White, *Excellence in Leadership*, p. 55.
6. White, *Excellence in Leadership*, p. 47.
7. Winston S. Churchill, *Their Finest Hour*, Vol. 2 of *The Second World War* (Boston: Houghton Mifflin, 1949), p. 25ff.
8. Boice, *Nehemiah: Learning to Lead*, p. 68.
9. White, *Excellence in Leadership*, p. 57ff.

CHAPTER 4: MAN-MANAGEMENT II: KEEPING GOING

1. Kidner, *Ezra and Nehemiah*, p. 82.
2. *Ibid.*, p. 83.
3. *Ibid.*, p. 90.
4. James Montgomery Boice, *Nehemiah: Learning to Lead*, p. 83.

CHAPTER 5: TESTED FOR DESTRUCTION

1. White, *Excellence in Leadership*, p. 83.
2. J. G. McConville, *Ezra, Nehemiah and Esther*, The Daily Study Bible, Old Testament, ed. John C. L. Gibson (Edinburgh: Saint Andrew Press and Philadelphia: Westminster Press, 1985), p. 101ff.
3. White, *Excellence in Leadership*, p. 89.
4. Boice, *Nehemiah: Learning to Lead*, p. 102ff.
5. White, *Excellence in Leadership*, p. 95ff.
6. *Ibid.*, p. 104.

CHAPTER 6: TIMES OF REFRESHING

1. Frederick Carlson Holmgren, *Israel Alive Again: A Commentary on Ezra and Nehemiah* (Grand Rapids, MI: Eerdmans and Edinburgh: Handsel Press, 1987).
2. Kidner, *Ezra and Nehemiah*, p. 13.
3. Pierre Berton, *The Comfortable Pew* (Toronto: McClelland and Stewart, 1965).
4. Cited from J.I. Packer, *A Quest for Godliness* (Wheaton, IL: Crossway Books, 1990), p. 97ff. John Rogers of Dedham was the preacher.
5. White, *Excellence in Leadership*, p. 111.
6. Kidner, *Ezra and Nehemiah*, p. 109.
7. Boice, *Nehemiah: Learning to Lead*, p. 194.

CHAPTER 7: BACK TO SQUARE ONE

1. White, *Excellence in Leadership*, p. 111.
2. Kidner, *Ezra and Nehemiah*, p. 129.
3. White, *Excellence in Leadership*, p. 131.
4. Kidner, *Ezra and Nehemiah*, p. 129.
5. For the case pro and con, see R. T. Beckwith and Wilfred Stott, *This is the Day* (London: Marshall, Morgan and Scott, 1978) (in U.S.: *The Christian Sunday: A Biblical and Historical Study* [Grand Rapids, MI: Baker Book House, 1980]); and, ed. D. A. Carson, *From Sabbath to Lord's Day: A Biblical, Historical, and Theological Investigation* (Grand Rapids, MI: Zondervan, 1982).
6. Barber, *Nehemiah and the Dynamics of Effective Leadership*; Swindoll, *Hand Me Another Brick*; White, *Excellence in Leadership*; Boice, *Nehemiah: Learning to Lead*.
7. Matthew Henry, *A Commentary on the Holy Bible* (1704-14), Preface to Nehemiah.
8. Kidner, *Ezra and Nehemiah*, p. 130.

EPILOGUE: TWO IMPOSTERS

1. Bryan Chapell, *Christ-centered Preaching* (Grand Rapids, MI: Baker, 1994), p. 282.

Index

Scripture Index